The
Seven Colors
of the Rainbow

Rabbi Yirmeyahu Bindman

Resource Publications, Inc.
San Jose, California

Editorial director: Kenneth Guentert
Managing editor: Elizabeth J. Asborno

© 1995 Resource Publications, Inc. All rights reserved. No
part of this book may be photocopied or otherwise
reproduced without written permission from the publisher.
For reprint permission, write to:

Reprint Department
Resource Publications, Inc.
160 E. Virginia Street #290
San Jose, CA 95112-5876

Library of Congress Cataloging in Publication Data
Bindman, Yirmeyahu.
    The seven colors of the rainbow : Torah ethics for
non-Jews / Yirmeyahu Bindman.
      p.   cm. — (Or l'amim)
    Includes index.
    ISBN 0-89390-332-9
    1. Noahide Laws. 2. Noahides. I. Title.
    BM520.73.B56 1995
    296.3'85—dc20   95-19163

Printed in the United States of America

99 98 97 96 95 | 5 4 3 2 1

Distributed to the general trade by Atrium Publishers Group.
Available from Baker & Taylor and Ingram.

Distributed to the Jewish trade by Feldheim Publishers.

CONTENTS

the connection to rapacious sex; the origin of steak tartare; modern slaughter customs; vegetarianism; the dispute between Joseph and his brothers; prohibition does not apply to fish; the question of eating blood; how animals benefit; relationship of this commandment to the color green.

The commandment to organize courts of justice; relationship of this commandment to malchut or "sovereignty"; this commandment is the purpose of government; judges are the key; courts come from the kings; rules for non-Jewish courts; rules of evidence; "unintentional" violations; breaking the law to save one's life; rules for judges; overthrowing rulers who break the law; execution of King Charles I; the Seven Laws return to England—and go to America; when justice can't be done; the Jewish New Year; repentance; relationship of this commandment to the color brown.

Special principles and supplementary commandments beyond the Seven Laws; acknowledging the Creator; human rulership over animal life; rules protecting animals; honoring parents; the redemption of Oscar Wilde; delaying justice, perverting justice, and teaching Torah incorrectly; the role of non-Jews in the redemption of the world; the judgment of heaven; Rosh Hashanah.

I

A mong all the nations of the world and all their religions, not one regularly offers anything to people who do not belong to that faith or nation. Each and every group says to others, "Join us, and do as we do, and then you can benefit from what we have. If you do not, then you are no concern of ours, beyond what we do of our own accord." Because the Jews do not seek to convert others to their own religion, most people assume that they are just happy to be left alone and that, if they had something to contribute to an average person's life, they would be trying to win new recruits to their cause.

Yet this is not the case. Behind the Jews' reluctance to turn other people into Jews, there is a full understanding of non-Jewish needs and a complete framework within which to satisfy those needs. The world is full of different ways and opinions, although everyone knows at heart that it is all one. Every nation has its own place in the sun, and every individual wants to follow his or her own destiny. In practice, though, this often leads to disharmony. The competing parties have too much at stake to become true allies. Something is still missing from their outlook, something to make it all hold together. The parties are alike in being non-Jewish, but no one would claim that non-Jewishness is only the negative state of not being a Jew, without any value or destiny of its own. This is not the claim of the Bible nor of the scholars of the Jewish tradition throughout history, today as always. But these two questions of Jewish and non-Jewish identity are linked, and one cannot be answered without the other.

Before any of us can know who we are, we must find out about our common origin in its truth. We see how and why humanity became divided into two distinct forms, the Jewish and the Gentile. We shall need to know what the Bible itself really is and not call it by that name, which means merely "book," but by the Hebrew word *Torah*, which means "teaching." Torah is the living source of truth and holds the key to the lives of all humanity, Jew and Gentile alike.

And even before this, one must know that there is a God, and that He is the origin and cause of everything; for all things that exist have causes, but He alone has no cause greater than Him.

The answers begin with history, the true history of the origins of humankind. There was a creation at a particular point in time, after the creation of time itself, which manifested the world in its completeness, prepared for people as we have always known them. They never lacked the upright posture, their intelligent faculties, and the human surroundings of houses and furniture and clothes. All of humanity descends only from human ancestors, without any origin at a lower level of accomplishment. At the time of the creation, after the world with all its life forms was ready, God formed and made a single man and woman, intended for marriage and the bearing of children. They were created as young adults, and at first they did not live on the physical plane as we know it, but in a higher spiritual state known as the Garden of Eden, where they were close to truth and wisdom and where all their needs were provided for. At this time God gave them six moral precepts to uphold. They were commanded to establish law in society, not to blaspheme by cursing the Creator, to worship nothing other than Him, not to steal or kill, and to refrain from forbidden sexual relations. They were also subject to the seventh precept, the prohibition of eating meat taken from a living animal, but since they were not then allowed to eat meat at all they were not in possession of this moral precept in the same sense as the others. They married there in the garden, and they were assured that they would remain forever on this high spiritual level, producing children like themselves, if only they would earn the merit of fulfilling one divine commandment: to refrain from eating the fruit of a particular tree of the Garden (Gen 2:16-17). Because this fruit had been placed outside their ownership, they would transgress the prohibition against theft if they appropriated it for food. Even though they were very wise, they were led through the limitations of their reasoning to eat of that fruit, and thus the evil which had existed separately from them beforehand became mixed in with their own nature. Their bodies assumed a more physical constitution, they lost many of the higher levels of their wisdom and beauty, and they were expelled from the Garden to work for their own maintenance, much as we do today. Nevertheless they retained the essential human attribute known as the "image of God": the human face and upright posture, the faculty of speech, and the intelligence to understand their Creator and to fulfill His wishes through moral conduct.

They were the ancestors of all humanity, both Jews and Gentiles, and they knew the wisdom of the Torah as the Jews have it today from the relatively high level that they still occupied. After entering into their new state, the man and the woman remained obligated to fulfill the six commandments they had been given in the Garden of Eden. If they departed from these precepts, they would be penalized, just as in a different sense they had been in the Garden. If, on the other hand, they kept them faithfully, they would receive reward. In particular, the observance of these commandments would have the benefit of bringing all of creation back toward the state of Eden so that it might be completely restored at a time when God would choose. Everything was left to the man and woman's free will so that they might earn merit by choosing the path of kindness and obedience. At this stage, they were still forbidden to eat meat as food, and thus the tooth structure of all humanity is clearly adapted for eating vegetables, being far different from that of meat-eating animals with long, sharp incisors. In the event they kept the commandments faithfully, they would depart this world with a clear conscience and a good name, cleansed of their first sin.

They produced many children, among whom were also wise men and women, but within a short time moral standards declined so sharply that the majority of people became wrongdoers, committing violent robbery, sexual misdemeanors, and acts of false worship, all breaches of the commandments given at the start. Although God had foreseen this, the actuality brought out His divine grief and regret over having created humankind, and He resolved to destroy His world and begin the creation over again. However, there was at this time, seven full generations after the first man and woman were created, still

4

one man who had kept the charge of upright conduct given to his ancestors and who was worthy to be spared. This was Noah, whose name derives from the Hebrew word for the "comfort" that he brought into the world. When this name is reversed it spells out the Hebrew word *chen,* meaning beauty or grace, as is written (Gen 6:8), "But Noah found grace in the eyes of God." This symmetry in the words is the key to the kind of beauty that he represented. Noah was a man of great wisdom. He studied the Torah. He was a prophet and a married man, whose wife and sons also shared his level of conduct. He became prophetically aware of God's intention to destroy all the rest of humanity by a great flood if they would not cease from their evil. God told Noah to save himself by building a large wooden vessel before the people of his generation over a long period of time, in the hope that by watching his efforts they would realize the truth and also be saved. But it was not so, and amid threats to Noah's life from the watchers, God led him and all his immediate family into the ark that he had built. Along with Noah and his family came breeding pairs of every animal that had refrained from the sexual perversions being committed at the time. God Himself shut them safely inside the ark before the rains began.

The purpose of the flood was to cleanse the earth itself from the effects of the sins through the spiritual nature of water, which under certain conditions forms a part of Jewish practice today. While the flood lasted, the planetary system and the rotation of the earth were held in abeyance so that there was no day and night—and no seasons. Noah and his three sons lived separated from their wives because of the prevailing distress and were occupied in prayer and study and in caring for the animals. Theirs was a miraculous environment in every sense, except that the ark itself and its provisions had been made by their own hands. They knew that they alone were to found the renewed state of life on earth, and they prepared themselves in righteousness for the responsibility. The ark was a complete "microcosm," a small entity that contained the elements of the whole creation within itself and, as such, it was a predecessor of the Temple at Jerusalem, a very high spiritual level where all of reality was gathered and dedicated to God.

When the waters of the flood retreated, the ark settled on the ground in the Caucasus mountains, and Noah and his sons emerged with their families. Noah built an altar at the Temple site in Jerusalem and offered sacrifice in thanksgiving for the deliverance and for the opportunity to start again. The Torah states that God "smelled the sweet odor of the sacrifice" (Gen 8:21), meaning that He was gratified that His will had indeed been carried out. At this point, God made a covenant with the whole creation that in the merit of Noah He would never again destroy it because of the sins of humanity. The rabbis say that at this moment Noah looked out from the ark upon a "new world," completely fresh and ready for him to build and to make his own, free from the threat which had hung over it. This freshness has never disappeared, and it is revealed anew after all the lesser troubles which have come upon humanity in later generations. God also gave to the people the right to eat meat, only stipulating that food animals be rendered completely dead before any part of them was eaten.

This last commandment given to Noah, together with the previous six, completed the "Seven Commandments" that became the universal law of humankind to this day. All non-Jews in the world, of every land and color, are heirs to Noah's achievement. All of humanity, diverse as it is, descends from the three sons of this one man, whose great scope made the foundation for them all. This covenant of everlasting life was given through the sign of the rainbow, which God told Noah would be the reminder in the heavens of His eternal decision. Now everyone need only to look up after a rain, and they can see the beautiful display that assures them that evil will never be allowed to overcome them. And God gave the rainbow seven distinct colors—to remind men and women of the Seven Commandments that lay behind the covenant, the laws that will bring all of humanity to merit their ultimate redemption.

II

At the stage following the flood, humanity was still one united body, speaking only the Hebrew language and living in one place, the area now known as Mesopotamia or Iraq, where the Tigris and Euphrates rivers flow through a fertile plain. Here the people had settled and given birth to children. Their state of security was so great that they began to consider themselves the masters of all creation, ready to challenge God Himself for supremacy. They saw their own unity as the key to this, and they did not commit the sins of banditry and sexual infidelity for which the previous generation had been condemned. They were kind and loving to one another, but they grew arrogant as a group and decided to build a high tower, the Tower of Babel, from which to gain an access to heaven.

This was a form of idolatry, and their punishment from the heavenly court was that their languages should be confused. They would no longer understand each other as before. This was the origin of separate languages as we now have them; seventy basic tongues were established, from which all of today's languages descended. This was also the number of the actual nations of the non-Jewish world before they were subdivided and intermingled. Thousands of words in English and other languages bear signs of Hebrew origin from this event, often with similarities where no known relationship exists between the other languages themselves. For example, the English word "direct" or "direction" has counterparts in fifteen other languages, as far apart as Gaelic *tu-rus*, Malay *da-ra*, and Russian *do-ro-ga*, all of which originate in the Hebrew word *derech*, meaning road or way.

Because of their newly acquired linguistic differences, the people began to quarrel over the building of the tower and they were forced to abandon the project. They decided to move away from this central place, and they re-assembled in different locations depending on which language they spoke. Thus, the families of the earth became settled in their separate locations. While this was going on, the Seven Laws in all their detail were being taught from an academy in Jerusalem established by Shem, the son of Noah, and his grandson Eber. Anyone who wanted was free to come and learn. However, various temptations and the distances between the peoples were increasing. Soon the nations developed idolatrous cults of their own, based on the mistake of early stargazers who thought that since the stars and planets were serving their Creator, it was proper to worship them instead of Him.

Shem and Eber were scholars of the whole Torah, as it is known to the Jews today, but in their time only the Seven Laws had actually been manifested as commandments for the people to observe and keep; the rest remained, as it were, "in heaven."

In these circumstances there arose the first wicked king, Nimrod of Ur, who forced all others to submit to him by making himself an actual object of worship. This was the first instance of a form of tyranny that has never since disappeared, a tyranny over the human spirit as it strives for truth and for the freedom to express it. The solution came through the efforts of one man, whose descendants developed into the Jewish people themselves, still today the prime target for all such wicked rulers. This man was Abraham, born in Ur into a family of idolaters, who arrived by his own reasoning at the conclusion that only the Creator Himself should be worshiped and served, and that His name must be made known to all humankind.

Nimrod tried to kill Abraham for speaking out against his ruling cult, but Abraham was miraculously saved. Then God told him to leave the land of his birth and to travel to "a land which I shall show you." This was the land of Israel, the Holy Land, which God gave to Abraham and his descendants as an inheritance, as a place in which to keep all of His commandments in the Torah and thus to be close to Him.

There Abraham studied at the academy of Shem and Eber, and he acquired great wisdom. He traveled with his wife and his flocks and herds, offering hospitality to people and discussing the concepts of divinity with them, each according to his level. Sarah, meanwhile, instructed the women. Abraham wrote books and devoted all his wealth to doing kindness to everyone who needed it. He brought them primarily to the Seven Laws, by which he himself was bound, but his efforts for the spreading of this awareness earned him a much higher reward; his descendants were to be given the privilege of keeping the whole Torah in the Jewish manner.

After they had passed many years without children, Abraham's first wife, Sarah, gave birth to Isaac, in whom

Abraham's wisdom and his blessings were to be continued. Sarah had previously allowed Abraham to take a second wife, Hagar, in order that he might have a son. Hagar gave birth to Ishmael, in whom Arab and Moslem leadership originated. Ishmael challenged Isaac for the entire succession; though he was not found worthy for this, his greatness continued, and he died righteous and esteemed.

Isaac continued Abraham's work in his turn, never leaving the Holy Land all his life. His son, Jacob, completed the original task by fathering twelve sons and taking them to live in Egypt at God's command. These twelve men became the fathers of the Jewish people. Jacob was also challenged for the succession by his twin brother, Esau. Western power and success, as dramatically revealed in the rise of the Roman Empire, originated in Esau. Jacob knew the unworthiness of Esau and captured his truth by impersonating him before their father, later also escaping his brother's revenge.

When Jacob brought his family to Egypt, the observance of the Seven Laws was not widespread. Egypt in particular was a sinful place where immorality had a status close to law. After Jacob's twelve sons died, the evil kings of Egypt, the pharaohs, set out to enslave the Jewish people, to destroy their spiritual and ethical concepts, and to restrict their independence of thought. Thus the situation remained for hundreds of years. But God saw their sufferings, and He remembered the relationship of divine love that He had made with Abraham, Isaac, and Jacob. At an appointed time, He brought them out of Egypt among great plagues and wonders, through the hand of the chosen prophet, Moses, whom He had found worthy to teach and to lead them.

Moses led the Jews out into the Sinai Desert, and they gathered at a small mountain where Moses ascended to God before the eyes of them all. He remained there receiving the whole Torah from God through his prophetic faculties, and then he came down to teach it to them. Thus, the Jewish people were established as they exist today, charged with keeping the entire body of the divine commandments.

This event took place in the year 1312 BCE (Before Common Era). At this time, during which the whole world was aware of what was happening, the state of the Garden of Eden was restored to humanity. (This state was to be lost again through other sins and errors of judgment.) The other nations were again given the Seven Laws that had been told to Noah, and the Jews were given the duty of teaching them. From then onward, all non-Jews who kept the Seven Laws were known by the Hebrew title of *Chasidei Umot ha-Olam* or "righteous of the nations."

Thus the Jews were brought out of the desert and restored to the land of Israel, the place whose nature was fit for wisdom and for the observance of Torah law. There they obeyed the commandments to set a king over themselves to rule according to the Torah and to build a Temple on the original altar site in Jerusalem for the offering of sacrifices as the law prescribed. In these ways they performed the task of linking all of earthly creation to its origin in heaven.

While the Jews lived on their land, with the Temple in their midst, they had a high level of spiritual awareness. Prophecy was a constant factor in their lives. These centuries also saw the rise of other empires: Greece, with its scientific and artistic excellence, and Persia and Babylon, with highly developed sorcery cults of a kind that has now disappeared. The Greek world produced many truly great thinkers, such as the philosopher Aristotle, but its cult of beauty also led many people to a self-indulgent way of life, immoral and idolatrous. Thus, inevitably, there were elements that came into conflict with Torah and the world of Jewish learning. During the early years of the Second Temple, these forces mounted an all-out campaign to conquer the land of Israel and to force the Jews away from the Torah. These Greeks opposed the Torah as much because of the Seven Laws as from any concern over the life led by the Jews themselves. They wanted to pollute Jewish wisdom with impure concepts to the point where it would lose the capacity to influence non-Jews in favor of Noachide practice. They sent troops into the Holy Temple itself in an attempt to destroy its altars and to contaminate the sacred olive oil used for lighting the lamps. This was no act of random destruction: this oil and its light correspond in the Temple service to the maintaining of pure Torah wisdom.

However, the *Cohanim*, the priestly branch of the Jewish nation who were devoted to the Temple service, rose in armed revolt against the invader. With divine help, they gained a military victory. On re-entering the Temple, they discovered one single flask of oil that had remained sealed against contamination. It contained only enough oil for one day, but they trusted in God. In a further miracle, the light lasted eight whole days until more pure oil could be prepared. This was the origin of the present-day Jewish festival of Chanukah, where lights are lit for eight days in perpetuation of the miracle.

The victory over the Greeks did not merely secure the Jewish nation against an invader but also restored Torah to its place and maintained the entire moral order of the world. The Jews had also won the ability to teach the Seven Laws without interference, and through the succeeding years their influence grew. A movement arose among Greeks and other nations to abandon Greek culture and seek Torah enlightenment instead. In Temple times, the non-Jews who formally took on the duty of observance of the Seven Laws were given the right to live in the land of Israel alongside the Jews, sharing in its divine insights and joys together with them. Both within the land and outside it they formed large communities in association with the synagogues. By the time of the rise of Imperial Rome they had become so prominent that the Roman government gave them special status in law, with the influence of their beliefs felt all across the empire.

They were known as "Godfearers," *yirei shamayim* in Hebrew. In Italy and other western regions of the empire they were called by the Latin equivalent *metuentes*. In the Greek-speaking lands to the east, where they were much more numerous, they were known as *phoboumenoi* (fearers of the One) or *theosebei* (worshipers of God). A memorial tablet found in the synagogue of Aphrodisias in Turkey in 1976, commemorating donors to charity, has two separate groups of names: one is of Jews, but the other is of Greeks, such as "Polychronios," "Apianos," and "Athenagoras," and it is headed with the words, "and also these Fearers of the One...."

A similar inscription has also been found in the synagogue of Sardis, this time with three groups of names: born Jews, full converts to Judaism, and observers of the Seven Laws. The "Fearers" are mentioned many times by the Roman commentators and historians, often with sarcasm and mockery of their closeness to the Jewish world and its ideas.

Josephus records how each city in Syria from which the emperor had expelled the Jews still had its population of Greek "sympathizers." He also describes the large non-Jewish community associated with the synagogue of Antioch, which was then one of the largest cities in the world. The biographer Plutarch, in his *Life of Cicero*, describes how the great lawyer-politician defended a free Roman accused of abandoning the pagan religion of the state in favor of "Jewish practices," making clear that the accused had not in fact become a Jew.

The satirists Petronius and Juvenal derided non-Jews who "act the part of the Jew," mocking at their reluctance to be circumcised even after accepting Jewish truth upon themselves. Talmudic sources speak of a non-Jewish king named Lemuel who was reproached by Rabbi Hanina for unseemly behavior with the reminder, "Your father was a Fearer of Heaven." The Noachide observers were often well-educated people, sometimes members of the Roman aristocracy, and they endured and answered the pagan wits with great patience and intellectual distinction. The Roman Emperor Antoninus, who enjoyed a close friendship with the Jewish sage Rabbi Judah the Prince, was thought to have established that relationship on the basis of a personal adherence to the Seven Laws. Josephus also mentions a King Izates, who underwent a Jewish "conversion" without being circumcised after discussions with a Jew named Ananias who lived within his kingdom of Adiabene in Mesopotamia. These Gentiles lived happy and fruitful lives, filled with the knowledge of truth, realizing their non-Jewish potential before the eyes of everyone.

It is often claimed that "ten percent of the empire" was Jewish, but the number of Jews who emerged from that period into more recent times does not bear out the contention that all these millions had converted in full. By far the majority of them were Noachide observers, non-Jews who had rejected paganism and formed an association with the Torah that gave them a status of their own.

These were times which saw a great moral development in the non-Jewish world, as the absurdity of the old pagan ways became obvious to everyone. Public and private morality became the dominant issue in people's lives, as it is to a great extent today. While the Jews were established in the Holy Land, with the Temple at its heart for all to see, there was no mistaking the source from which the necessary ideas had to come. Similar developments were taking place also in the Persian Empire, and even in India and China, because the fame and glory of the Temple were known in all parts of the world. At this time the Hindu religion was led away from its early idolatry toward acknowledging the single Creator as it does today. The Buddhist ideology also arose to take the Far East onto a higher level than it had known before.

As these developments proceeded, the Roman state became the scene of a considerable struggle between non-Jews who stood fast by the Seven Laws and early church leaders who wanted the public to settle for a new religion that was based on Jewish themes but incorporated elements of Greek idolatry into its framework. The writing of the New Testament in Greek, based on the deeds of a certain Jew who had believed himself linked to messianic concepts, was intended to further the aim of the latter group. When the church made its bid for official domination, it was offering to reconcile the widespread desire for idolatrous concepts with the equally widespread desire for pure truth.

In time, there was a clear division between these two tendencies at all levels of life and politics. At its peak the struggle led to the brief but eventful reign of the Emperor Julian, known to Christian history as "the Apostate." He was a remarkable man, only twenty-four years old when he came to the imperial throne in the year 361, determined to give a moral basis to the crisis-ridden government in a very short span of time.

Julian was a cousin of the emperor, raised far away from the Roman court surroundings, and his early education had been mainly in Greek philosophy. Though he was considered an outsider in Roman politics, or perhaps because of it, the Emperor Constantius recognized his keen intelligence and gave him an important military command in the war against the tribes in what is now Germany. Against all the odds, he succeeded in battle and aroused the jealousy of the emperor, who ordered him recalled.

Julian's friends in Rome, aware of his moral and intellectual potential, rose up in revolt when they heard of his recall and proclaimed him emperor. Before the situation could develop into a full-scale civil war, Constantius died, leaving Julian as his only legitimate successor. The young man came to the throne with no ties to any of the powerful established forces of the state, whose greed and arrogance were tearing the fabric of society apart. His philosophical training had brought him close to Jewish ideas and to the Seven Laws at the exact time when their relevance was greatest.

Though the Christian bishops were pressing hard for their faith to become the sole official doctrine, Julian refused them and proclaimed constitutional freedom of religion. He allowed pagan temples to function, along with synagogues and Christian churches, but his policy in government was based on spiritual values that were intended to raise the tone of life above the level of interfaith competition. He reduced the taxes that burdened the working people and kept inflation down by banning price rises and stemming the flow of gold across the empire's borders. He completed the war with the aggressive German tribes, realizing that the state would never become stable until its borders were secure. The support of the "Godfearers" maintained his prestige, and the quality of the social fabric began to improve.

However, the senatorial class soon felt their privileges were being threatened, and the church sought to win them over as allies for the Christian cause. Propaganda was spread among the poor, alleging that the Jews and their adherents were planning to exploit them even more, and this was helped by the power which Julian's policies had given to the bureaucrats who administered the reforms. Within two years the emperor's position was under threat; he had gone for high moral stakes, but the empire itself was so unstable that chaos had risen against him.

In order to win final military security, he led an army to the east against the Persian Empire, the last strong power that posed a danger to Rome. His legions reached the Persian capital itself, going further than Roman armies had ever gone before. However, he retreated from the task of mounting a siege in the heat of summer. As the army marched away, he was hit by a stray arrow and died on the sand. Thus fell the last official advocate of the Seven Laws until modern times, a man whose courage was brooked only by the most elemental forces that menace the rule of law.

III

Nearly two thousand years ago, the Roman Empire conquered the land of Israel and brought to an end the Jewish statehood that the kings had founded. The Roman troops rioted and burned down the Temple for revenge and for its treasures in silver and gold. The Romans deported many of the Jewish inhabitants, including the wise rabbis who provided the teaching and the interpretation of the Torah. This was the start of the worldwide Jewish exile that has lasted until our own time. The exile will end completely when the Messiah, the heir to the original kings of the house of David, is brought out from obscurity to rebuild the Temple and to reign again in Jerusalem.

After the Jews were exiled, it became much more difficult for Gentiles to gain instruction on the Seven Laws or to keep them. Conditions for Jews became dangerous, even the teaching of the Torah sometimes being banned, and it was almost impossible for Gentiles to leave the surroundings where these penalties originated and find Jews willing to teach them. The Seven Laws had gone into exile also; some of the Godfearers actually became Jews, but most found the difficulties of their position too great without a secure Jewish community to support them. Like other non-Jewish people, they or their children tended to assume that Christianity, with its admixture of Torah concepts, would offer at least a little satisfaction. Through the fall of the Roman Empire and the rise of the kingdoms of the Middle Ages, these conditions continued. Only a few exceptionally courageous people were willing or able to find the Seven Laws for themselves.

The Christian and Moslem kingdoms came into armed conflict with each other, with war loss and danger an everyday occurrence, and Jews were unable to fulfill their duty of teaching in circumstances of open risk to their lives. A non-Jew who converted to Judaism in full would surely have to flee from danger, but at the end he would have the Jewish society to join. One who remained content with his non-Jewish identity under the Seven Laws would face just as much risk without any such solution.

However, on many occasions, the church and its officials were called upon to deal with "Judaizing" tendencies among the population. Similar phenomena also occurred in Moslem countries. A preacher would recommend that people abandon the official religion in favor of conforming to Jewish belief or practice in some way. Some would listen to him and do as he said, and soon the inquisitional machinery would be mobilized with terrible effect, often also against the Jews themselves for allegedly spreading contrary ideas.

The Albigensian or Cathar movement in early France tried to purge the prevailing non-Jewish religion of idolatry. Later, the Taborite and Hussite campaigns in Bohemia were motivated by the same basic principle. In nineteenth-century Russia, when the presence of Jews first began to attract the attention of the people at large, the Subbotniki were persecuted by the tsars for "Judaizing." Learned Jews understood that the root of these misguided movements lay in the instinctive desire of non-Jewish people to observe the Seven Laws. Unfortunately, in the threatening surroundings of exile, there was nothing Jews could do to help. They had to attend to their own safety.

Only when the wars of the Reformation began to discredit the crusading outlook altogether did the atmosphere begin to improve. Ideas of bettering the government and extending individual freedom gained ground among kings and citizens who had no more time or money for such expeditions. When the Thirty Years War destroyed the old Catholic order, plunging Europe into an almost mindless chaos of bloodshed and illegality, the church and the governments were left without prestige. A new basis for law had to be found from morality itself. And so the burnings of Jewish books, which took place in the Middle Ages, gave way to a new interest in Hebrew learning among non-Jews. It was not long before the leading thinkers began to encounter the Seven Laws once more.

This dialogue took place mostly in Holland, where Jewish refugees from Spain became close to the Dutch citizens who had fought to expel the Spanish governors from their tiny country. Rabbinic scholars discussed with the Dutch all the issues that confronted them in establishing their small state and securing its prosperity. Artists such as Rembrandt joined in this discussion also, painting many portraits of the rabbis themselves. Great legal minds assembled at the universities. They taught and wrote on the principles and philosophy of law, and they began to codify the legal tradition out of the mass of legal precedents that had come down from the Middle Ages. Among these were the English jurist John Selden (1584-1654) and the Dutch legal philosopher Hugo de Groot (1583-1645), known by the Latin name of Grotius. Selden was a Hebraist, a non-Jew who knew the Hebrew language and read the Jewish source-books in the original to learn their contents. He was not a Talmudic scholar, but he knew the works of the rabbis well, and he accepted their moral authority. He wrote a complete exposition of the Seven Laws for the scholars of his time in his Latin work, *De jure naturali et gentium, juxta disciplinium ebraorum* ("On natural and Gentile law, compared with Hebrew principles").

Selden began the seventh chapter of his book:

> *Sextum juris Noachidarum...quod de judiciis est,*
> *atque enumerationem ex Talmudicis aliquot.*
>   *Quod igitur in enumeratione illa Septumum est,*
> *"eber min ha-chai," quo crudelitas immanis in*
> *animalia cetera vetatur.*

> Six of the Noachide laws, those of judicial significance, are enumerated first in the Talmud among other sources.
>   The seventh is therefore the prohibition of "the limb of a living animal," which forbids cruelty to animals.

Grotius laid the foundations of modern international law in his *De jure belli ac pacis* ("On the rights of war and peace"), where he quoted the leading Rabbinic writers extensively as sources for the universal morality. He wrote:

> In the Hebrew sources we find of the "pious ones of the Gentiles," as the Talmud describes them. These, as the Jewish teachers themselves declare, are bound

to observe the laws given to Adam and Noah, to
abstain from idols, from blood, and from other things
which will be mentioned further.

In this way the Seven Laws were brought once more
into the foundations of non-Jewish life, helping to form
the ideas with which the western world led humankind
into the modern era. Men of learning became the founders of states based on morality, owing little to the
prejudices which had gone before. Their assimilation of
Torah concepts made it inevitable that the Jews themselves would later be emancipated and freed from legal
segregation.

Dutch rabbis also negotiated the readmission of the
Jews into England on terms involving the Seven Laws.
The leaders of the English republic were less committed
to the principles then the Dutch had been, but they
reached an agreement satisfactory enough to begin Jewish life in the west as we know it today.

When the United States of America was established,
as the first new state designed according to these principles from the outset, non-Jewish people began to sense
the new conditions and to show renewed interest in the
Jews who, though now free from official hostility, were
still exiled among them.

Questions began to be asked of the Jews: why do
you maintain your separate identity? what interests do
you serve? where do you go from here if this is not where
you truly belong? and what is your purpose here if your
destiny is only to leave?

These were legitimate questions, and they needed
answers. Because the Jews, only newly released from
restrictive ghetto surroundings, were often eager to pass
undistinguished from their non-Jewish neighbors, the
answers were often hard to find. But some were able to

find them. The nineteenth-century German Rabbi Samson Rafael Hirsch, who was then the leader of the only large Jewish community living in free and affluent circumstances, gathered non-Jews quietly around him for study and wrote on the concept of the Seven Laws in his books and letters. Other questing personalities also managed to reach the goal. One of these was a young Frenchman named Aimé Pallière, who in the year 1900 had a series of conversations with the Rabbi of Leghorn (Livorno) in Italy on what religious path he should choose. They corresponded by letter, exchanging questions and ideas, and between them they set out the whole path for the rediscovery of the Seven Laws in modern times. We ourselves can begin to understand our own situation in its truth when we read the words that passed between Rabbi Elijah Benamozeg and his pupil Aimé Pallière.

IV

orn in 1879 in Lyons, France, Aimé Pallière grew
up from early childhood seeking truth through
religious expression, and his surroundings led
him to feel a call to join the Roman Catholic priesthood.
A man with an inquiring mind, he tried to find the deeper
meaning of everything that he encountered. His examination of the basic Christian texts led him to believe that
something was amiss. A word like "virgin" bore a different meaning in Christian translation than it had in the
Hebrew from which it derived. He looked further, and
he found no solution.

He was a religious man, who had been brought up
in a Catholic atmosphere, and now fundamental Catholic
dogmas were presenting him with problems. What was
he to do? His first response was to join the Protestant
fold. The Salvation Army, based in England, was begin-
ning to establish small missions in the industrial cities of
France. Like many people at that time, Pallière saw the
evils of working-class slum existence as the most pressing
problem of all, and the Salvation Army was trying to do
something. He began mission work in Lyons, but again
he was disappointed. The Salvation Army meant well,

but he felt there was something about their basic doctrine that left them at a loss when dealing with ordinary people.

What was that "something?" All his observations led him to conclude that it was the "Trinity," the item of belief by which Christianity separates itself from all others. At this time, he became acquainted with Jews from the small Lyons community, and he realized that theirs was a religion with no such concept to distract the mind. There was one God alone, and the only service was that related directly to Him. He studied Torah and, gratified by what he learned, he made up his mind to become a Jew himself. After all, this was the faith in which all the others originated, and it was the meanings in the Hebrew text that had led him to question what he had first been told.

When he found out more of the details of the conversion process, he became discouraged once more. The convert to Judaism had to abandon his previous non-Jewish identity altogether, acquiring an entirely new personal nature like that of all other Jews in order to approach the fulfillment of the whole Torah.

Pallière did not question the need for this, but he was not at all sure what the effect would be on himself. He was deeply attached to his mother, and he had many other relatives and friends to whom he was closely linked. How could he separate himself from all of this? Was it worth nothing in the scale of truth? And his mind was forming an even more important question, one that placed him on an original level in his own time: Why, indeed, if only the Jewish faith was the true one, had God created him as a non-Jew in the first place?

His Jewish friends saw his dilemma, and they realized the honesty with which he was seeking his true path. They made inquiries on his behalf, and they came up with a name and an address which gave hope of solving the problem. Over the southern border of France, at Leghorn in Italy, there was an ancient community of Sephardi Jews whose ancestors had fled there from the Spanish Inquisition. The rabbi of that community, Elijah Benamozeg, was a senior scholar and writer with a wide education and a liberal mind.

Pallière wrote to him, asking for a meeting. On arriving in Leghorn, Pallière received a note saying that the rabbi was coming to greet him at the small hotel where he was staying. This personal approach, far removed from hierarchy or protocol, made a great impression on Pallière, who knew he was much younger than the rabbi. This was confirmed when a knock on the door of his room announced a most ordinary-looking old man, bearded and stooping, with conventional clothes and a ready smile.

In *The Unknown Sanctuary*, written many years later, Pallière described what followed. The rabbi listened to him explain his doubts about becoming a Jew, and the rabbi acknowledged them all. He told Pallière that there was no duty on anyone's part to become a Jew, and that the anguish his mother might feel on being parted from her son was certainly not misplaced. He went on:

> We Jews have in our keeping the religion destined for the entire human race, the religion to which the Gentiles are subject and by which they are to be saved, as were our Patriarchs before the giving of the Law. Could you suppose that the true religion which God destines for all humanity is only the property of a special people? Not at all. His plan is much greater than that. The religion of humanity is no other than "Noachism," not because it was founded by Noah, but because it was through the person of that

righteous man that God's covenant with humanity was made. This is the path that lies before your efforts, and indeed before mine, as it is my duty to spread the knowledge of it also.

Rabbi Benamozeg explained that the present non-Jewish religions acknowledged their origins in Judaism but were not prepared to admit that Judaism was still what it had always been, preferring to insist that the Jews should convert out of their ancestors' faith.

"They are founded on the principle of the abolition of the Torah even for the Jews," he told the Frenchman, "and they ignore in the Jewish prophets all that you yourself have known so well how to find in them."

Pallière was transfigured by what he had heard. The elderly rabbi had told him that a great and far-reaching concept existed where he had thought there was nothing at all. There was a place for the non-Jew who realized Jewish truth but could not become a Jew. He had never heard of a religion which offered something to those who were not entirely a part of it, and he realized immediately that only the Jewish faith possessed the expanded views, and the humility, to make such an offer. Rabbi Benamozeg saw the effect of his words, and he added:

> The future of the human race lies in this formula. If you come to be convinced of it, you will be much more precious to Israel than if you submit to the Torah of Israel. You will be the instrument of the Divine Providence to all mankind. If you were a skeptic like so many others, you might as well preach one doctrine as another, but you have earned the right that I should speak to you as a believer.

He smiled, and continued: "I am surprised that I have expressed myself so freely, but it is proof of my sincerity, and of the deep interest that you have inspired in me."

Such words change the whole course of the life of a man. Pallière took his leave, and the two never met again, but until the rabbi's death three years later, the two men exchanged letters carrying forward the suggestion that had been made and accepted.

Pallière had to face the task of adapting his life to a set of beliefs that he alone knew and understood, and it was not surprising that his confidence did not immediately jump to the level that was needed. He wrote, "Not to be a Christian, not to be a Jew and yet after a fashion to adopt Judaism, was an equivocal position which in that state of faith had little attraction for me."

He expressed his indecision in letters to the rabbi, who replied at length with the aim of helping his pupil to face the challenges of the new position:[1]

> If I understand you correctly, "Noachism" seems to
> you a far distant and superannuated thing, and you
> ask how after the passing of so many centuries of
> progress I can dream of taking you back to the
> foundations of worship that existed after the Flood.
> Is this possible? Yes it is, and I trust you will soon
> see that its future prospects likewise would not be
> possible if they had not also been present so far in
> the past.
>
> The "Noachic" religion is not a contrivance nor an
> invention. It is an established fact, discussed on every
> page of our Talmud, and our wise men generally
> admit that it is little known and much misunderstood.
>
> According to the teachings of Judaism the Jews as
> the "priests" of humanity are subject to the Law of
> Moses, while the "laymen" are linked to the early

1
The quotations throughout the rest of this chapter are portions of letters reprinted in *The Unknown Sanctuary*.

universal religion alone. Christianity on the other hand introduced confusion into this, by either imposing the Law on the Gentiles through James, or abolishing it for the Jews through Paul.

Rabbi Benamozeg answered Pallière's heartfelt query about the importance of the non-Jewish identity:

> Can it be imagined for a single moment that after having concerned Himself for so long with the descendants of Noah, God would give a special Law to the Jews as His "kingdom of priests" and then not trouble Himself further about the rest of the human race? Would He thus leave them totally abandoned, without revelation and without law, abolishing His ancient Noachide bond with them, so that they must rely for long centuries on their own poor reason? Not even a mortal man would behave in such a way.

He went further, explaining the manner in which the Talmudic masters expounded the detailed provisions of the Seven Laws.

> You will find there in abundance the complete elements of the code that you are seeking, and you who know Hebrew can convince yourself of it without difficulty. If one takes into account the circumstances in which the Sages discussed these questions, threatened with dire penalties even for teaching to their own people, their words unmistakably bear the Divine seal. They make an impression on the faith and the admiration of everyone, they rise to heights that even you do not dream of; it is Rabbinic Judaism and its authorized interpreters, the princes of wisdom and dedication.

Pallière was convinced. He continued on his path and eventually came into positions of responsibility in both the Jewish and non-Jewish worlds that no one else had ever held at the same time. He earned the love and respect of all who came into contact with him. For the rest of his life, the memory of his dialogue with Rabbi Benamozeg inspired him. He described the meaning that it held for him in the personal sense.

> One cannot sufficiently admire the way in which the master used language that a young Catholic would understand. But what was even more remarkable was that he was not merely assuming a position for the occasion, because of the nature of the argument; he was giving his beliefs an exact expression. And I say simply that no human being ever spoke to me as he did.

The Rabbi had given him the comfort he needed when he wrote,

> Why do you speak of feelings of isolation? I see all around you a great multitude of believers. I grant you that the outward signs may not be visible, but nevertheless you will truly be of the community of your brethren, the community of the future. For this, according to the Jews, is the true religion of the Messianic times.

Now Pallière knew who and what he truly was, and many people came to know of how Torah applied to non-Jews through his example. But the world around him was afflicted with evils, turning toward the turmoil of the First World War, the Russian Revolution, and the rise of Nazi power. The Jews were facing the terrible challenge of modern machine persecution, and he alone could not lead the non-Jewish peoples out of their situation. During the Nazi occupation of France, he was compelled to stop his work for fear of the Gestapo, but they did not come to harm him of their own accord. Hitler had no idea what he represented and therefore was not afraid of him. He died in 1949, beloved by everyone who had known him, leaving his writings and his example to those who would come after. We who do so may now see clearly what was the faith that had earned his devotion.

V

Our world is based so firmly on the concept of freedom that nothing seems so problematic as the idea of a "commandment." We are not given any easy way to understand an instruction to do something which we have not already decided upon and which we may not even fully understand. It seems like a return to the days before modern education, when social structures were rigid and people were unable to determine their own destinies or improve their situation.

The people of earlier times were certainly not stupid or backward. Their technical development was less than ours, but their philosophical level was higher than ours because they were closer to the early period of great Torah scholarship and prophecy. Nevertheless, they had to contend with much wrong thinking and superstition, some of it deliberately fostered by those in authority. The modern way of life, based on individual liberty and integrity, was in many ways a tremendous improvement. The opportunity to think for oneself and to arrive at a suitable way of life was a precious thing, even if the certainties of the old way of life had to be re-examined. And, since righteous truth is unchanging and eternal, it was only to be expected that honest people like Aimé Pallière would in the end discover it for themselves once more.

This, then, is the position of our own generation. People have come to realize that there exists a truth necessary for their lives, not distant from them in a transcendental way or held by only one group of devotees, but near to them, ready to be adopted and acted upon. All they need is a way to name these principles and a way to act them out in their lives. Once these principles are accepted and acted upon with faith, then the true wisdom behind them will be revealed and understood.

The innovation that the Seven Laws provide, the key to understanding all the challenges and hopes of the human situation, is simple. It is to know that one is "commanded," that there exist moral laws which the Creator has provided for His creatures, and that if one obeys these Divine commandments, one becomes bound up with His higher intelligence, which is the source of all peaceful solutions. With this knowledge, one becomes liberated from the troubles and contradictions of this world.

The list of prohibitions seems at first like a negative code, but in fact it is a "Bill of Rights," opening the way to true liberty and advancement. The United States congressional resolution on the Seven Laws, which former U.S. President George Bush signed into law on March 20, 1991 (H.J. Resolution 104, Public Law 102-14), recognized this when it described them as "the bedrock of all civilization." When law becomes a means to opportunity, when it offers progress instead of restriction, then it deserves to be obeyed. The Seven Laws offer these benefits as and when they are obeyed.

Western society has for a long time been regarded as "Christian," just as eastern societies have been considered "Moslem" or "Buddhist." But the true lives of western and eastern peoples are not at all so easily categorized. The dominant religions contain moral elements that their societies value highly, but they exclude other approaches and claims, often to the point of declaring war on them. Some of those moral claims are quite valid, while others are less pure and more self-justifying. Beyond the formal doctrines of the dominant religions are the associated folk traditions and ways of life, remnants of older religions that have been suppressed. These folk elements cannot be made to fit into the official systems, but they show the limitations of Christianity and other non-Jewish religions.

This true non-Jewish humanity, which sprang once more to the center of attention when America was founded on liberty, has now become the usual way of life for the peoples of the world. They want peace and love, they treat one another with dignity and are offended by inconsideration, they are aware that sexual life in particular has a fundamental significance that is not subject to human rules, and they regard most present-day religious claims as misleading.

Today, the non-Jewish personality is emerging in a way that has not been seen since the destruction of the Temple in Jerusalem forced the Jewish people into exile and their own Torah reality into hiding. Non-Jews are waiting for the truth that will answer their basic questions honestly and straightforwardly. They are ready for the Seven Laws, which state directly what is expected from non-Jews and what they can expect to receive in return.

Aimé Pallière, in his conversations with Rabbi Benamozeg in that small Italian hotel, discovered that the

Jewish truth had indeed survived all the centuries of hardship; its scholars were still trustworthy men of insight and concern, and they had something definite to offer any sincere person who came to them, whatever his or her origin might be.

Now that the shadows of Nazism and Communism have all but passed away from the world, leaving the Jewish people established in Israel and in other countries that respect their right to uphold their truth, the opportunity has come for them to do their duty to the other nations among whom they live. The western world is at peace, ready to listen to words of peace. Even the Middle East does not have to remain in a state of war once the intended relationship between Jew and non-Jew becomes established.

In the modern technical world of today, many pressures work against religious belief and practice, all of them tending to leave people in an uncertain, deficient position. Personal life has its human shortcomings, and music and other entertainment cannot make up for everything. When the stresses of modern life affect a person's well-being, he or she can seek therapy. Psychotherapists readily admit they serve the "confessor" function previously performed by ministers and priests, but their methods are rarely useful. They are trying to formulate an idea of the soul along scientific lines, but since the soul is above this level there is no relief by such means, apart from the help of individual good intentions.

The pioneer psychologist Dr. Carl Jung of Switzerland, a world-famous therapist who treated thousands of people over a lifetime career, stated that every one of them was suffering in some way from a lack of what religion gave to its believers. Even those who remain involved in religion, whether formal or simply personal and unstated, seem to sense that there is a level beyond which the regularly known ways cannot go.

The Seven Laws are simple in outline, clear and sensible to any person. No training in philosophy or theology is needed to understand them or to fulfill the morality they contain. Detailed interpretations are available in the rabbinic writings. In this deeper analysis is great wisdom, and this is something non-Jews may go into as much as they desire. The Seven Laws provide all that is required for the moral existence of the non-Jew, without the need for any other changes in philosophy, in the system of government, or any scientific discovery.

When we explore the commandments one by one, we shall see human society in a new light—or rather, in a light that has been all but hidden for a long time. There will be many revelations of how things might have been, and of how they still may be when they are seen from the perspective of eternal truth. Neither Jews nor non-Jews are meant to function in the material world alone, without a hint of where they come from, where they are going, and why they are here.

The laws of nature keep the inanimate world moving in its path, and we who have a will of our own are likewise given the laws of humanity, the moral laws which lift men and women from the natural level and unite them with the divine. And, like the colors of the rainbow, the moral laws are seven in number.

VI

All seven of the Noachide Laws are derived from specific passages in the Torah, mostly in the Book of Genesis, which tells the stories of Adam and Noah and relates the commandments given to them. Ultimately, they all originate from a single verse: Genesis 2:16. The later rabbinic authorities who explain these derivations dispute a number of points. Legal debate is the norm in rabbinic Judaism because truth is understood not as something clear and simple but as something diverse and many-sided. We shall see how the competing interpretations of the Noachide Laws serve to cover a much wider range of human possibilities.

The seven major headings, as mentioned before, are prohibitions against:

- sexual misconduct
- murder
- theft
- idolatry
- blasphemy

- eating live meat

- failing to establish courts of law

Under these headings come many detailed provisions, some directly inferred by the rabbis and others left to the individual to decide for himself or herself in accordance with the spirit of the laws. This is because the intention is not to punish offenders in any legalistic way but to show, by the means of specifying what is forbidden or frowned upon, what should be done for the best in any of life's contingencies.

For example, the prohibition against idolatry serves by contrast to affirm true belief and worship; the prohibitions on certain sexual relationships points to a desired situation that has no moral liabilities; the commandment to establish justice points to the need for a legal system, which every society requires for its functioning, even in so complex an environment as our own.

The intention of these commandments is not to render people guilty but to lead them in a way of truth that will make them happy and secure. This is a world in which decent people are often subjected to erroneous claims that have been accepted as true simply because no one can prove them wrong. We have a powerful need for clear moral laws that know no social or racial barriers and that apply to the great and mighty as much as to the small. Only this specific divine code of practice, ordained by God Himself out of His care for the world, without any myth or other motive, can provide this need without falling into the state of divisiveness produced by other attempts at prescription.

There is no need or obligation for a non-Jew to become a Jew in order to reach this level. A non-Jew who is accepted for conversion to Judaism leaves the

Seven Laws behind and can never return from the full Jewish obligations to observe the Noachide obligations alone. As specified in the Torah, conversion is accomplished by immersing the whole body in the pool of water known as a *mikveh*, before Jewish witnesses, with the stated intention to take on the observance of all 613 commandments.

On rising again from the water, the whole spiritual constitution of the person is changed to the Jewish nature. A male must also undergo circumcision beforehand. A non-Jewish child who is immersed along with a converting parent may relinquish the Jewish nature on reaching adulthood and become a non-Jewish observer of the Seven Laws once more. A non-Jew who wishes to keep the Seven Laws after becoming aware of them has no need of any ceremony. However, non-Jews may consolidate their position by affirming their wish to keep the Seven Laws before three scholars of the Torah.

Jewish tradition contains an element that, until the last few centuries, was taught only to the very wise. This "secret" wisdom, known as "Kabbalah" from the Hebrew word for "received" truth, outlines the way in which God formed and ordered the world. The Kabbalah can help a person understand the mysteries behind the creation. Its basic premise is the doctrine of the "Ten Sefirot," the ten divine emanations that carry God's original attributes into the structures that He created, both of the universe and of the human form.

When God desired to create the world for His truth and goodness, He did so by "projecting" these ten essential attributes into a "space" that He had made and ordering them in a way that would show His true purpose to the inhabitants whom He placed there. This He did through making the ten statements of the words "and

God said" in the Book of Genesis. The world actually consists of His divine speech, found in the Hebrew letters, and is different from human speech in that it lasts continually.

As we have seen, the human being is described in the Torah as being made in the "image of God," with a face containing two eyes, a nose and a mouth, and with a body, two legs and two arms. This arrangement is so fundamental, reflecting so much of divine truth and intentions, that in the Kabbalah it becomes the source for understanding almost the whole scheme of creation with its interrelationships and its destiny.

Three of the Sefirot, the first in order of descent from Him, are known as "intellectual":

- wisdom

- understanding

- knowledge

These in turn lead into the remaining seven "emotional" attributes:

- kindness

- strength

- beauty

- eternity

- glory

- foundation

- sovereignty

The Seven Laws are each signified by one of the seven emotional Sefirot, which derive their sustenance from the higher intellectual faculties.

This division also parallels the form of the human body:

- Kindness is signified by the right arm and Strength by the left.

- Beauty, which results from the proper blending of Kindness and Strength, corresponds to the torso with all the different organs the body requires.

- Eternity and Glory, which operate as a pair, signify the two thighs as they support the body each in turn.

- Foundation is represented by the male sexual organ, from which the new generations derive.

- Sovereignty, the lowest aspect but the most fundamental of all, is signified by the feet upon which the whole body stands.

There is also a connection to the seven colors of the rainbow; each Sefirah is associated with a single color representing its nature, some obvious and others requiring deeper examination. The number seven is likewise connected with the seven days of the week, since this signifies the complete natural cycle that underlies and fulfills the world in which we live. (There are other associations with the number seven—too many, however, to describe here.)

The Sefirot are not entities in any sense. They have no size or location, no intelligence or power. In essence, they are not individual because each contains within itself all the others.

Their names are those that Torah gives to God's own attributes and intentions—to the extent that He wishes to make them known—so that the human ear and mind can comprehend what is far above their capability: the mysteries of creation, whose truths are known only to the Creator Himself.

In this way, the Sefirot serve as signs for us to direct our efforts, Jews and non-Jews each according to the commandments we are given. The Sefirot represent the positive values damaged by breaches of the laws they parallel. Therefore, when the laws are upheld, the Sefirot shine forth, as it were, in their true goodness and purity, radiating the light of God's all-embracing love into the lives of humanity and blessing every aspect of existence above and below.

VII

The first of the Seven Laws from the Kabbalah perspective is the commandment to refrain from forbidden sexual relations. This corresponds to the Sefirah of *Chessed* or "Kindness." Thus, the commandment gives us to understand that forbidden sexual contacts are in fact the perversion of kindness and love.

In the Song of Songs, the Torah describes the experience of God's love with the words: "Let His right hand embrace me" (Song of Songs 2:6). In chapter VI, we noted that the Sefirah of Kindness corresponds to the "right arm." Thus, when we fulfill the conditions that God has set for our love to be pleasing to Him, relating through the categories that He chose when He formed and made us, then He will "embrace" us, showing the reality of His divine attribute of Kindness to us in our own lives.

This commandment for the non-Jew is derived from the famous passage spoken to Adam and Eve when they were created as a pair, "Therefore shall a man leave his father and mother, and cleave to his wife, and they shall be one flesh" (Gen. 2:24). From this one passage, we learn that there is:

- a prohibition against incest. The phrase "leave his father and mother" indicates that the child is not to interbreed with parents or their line;

- a prohibition against adultery and male homosexuality. A man is to "cleave to his wife" and not to another man's wife nor to another male;

- a prohibition against sexual relations by women or men with animals. The phrase "and they shall be one flesh" implies that the aim of sexual relations is to produce children of our own species in whom the man and woman become "one flesh."

The many other passages in the Torah dealing with sexual prohibitions, including "you shall not commit adultery" from the Ten Commandments, establish the rules which govern the Jews. Non-Jewish relations are conducted on an entirely different basis, and this is in itself one of the reasons why Jews and non-Jews are forbidden to each other. For sexual purposes all non-Jews have exactly the same status, and they may marry anyone they choose, whatever their race or social origin or nationality. When we look more closely at the rules for non-Jews, we may see how well the Torah appreciates their needs, how deep is its understanding of their situation.

The relationships forbidden to non-Jews are much fewer than for the Jewish people. For example, Jews may not have sexual relations with the progeny of either their mother or their father. For non-Jews, the prohibition against incest applies only to the progeny of the mother—even though non-Jews derive their family name from their fathers and inherit their father's property according to Torah law. Thus a non-Jewish man and woman with different mothers and the same father are not brother and sister, and they may marry each other just like any other partners.

A non-Jew is forbidden his own mother, his daughter because of her similar status to his mother, and the sisters of his father and mother. He is also barred from relations with his father's wife (not his mother), his brother's wife, his wife's sister (all these sibling relationships through the mother only), and his daughter-in-law and stepdaughter. The early authorities dispute over whether these prohibitions still apply after the father or brother has died. In addition to the regular ban on intercourse with a male, there is a special prohibition against relations with a father or brother.

Non-Jews are not commanded by the Torah to marry, so the prohibition against sexual misconduct does not make them liable for extra-marital relations within the permitted degrees. However, they are encouraged to marry, to be faithful to their chosen partner, and to have children. This encouragement to marry is an example of morality and kindness in human relations that goes beyond the actual provisions of the law—namely, that it is hurtful and unjust to have sexual relations without the protection of marriage and without constructing a suitable home environment in which children can be raised. For reasons of this kind, a decree was made by Shem, the son of Noah, together with his court, that forbade extra-marital relations from that time onward.

A Jew who is born of an incestuous or adulterous relationship is debarred from marrying into the rest of the Jewish community, but there is no similar concept of personal illegitimacy contained in the Seven Laws.

Jews have a commandment to marry and to produce children. While non-Jews have no such positive commandment, neither is any benefit attached to celibacy for religious purposes or any others. It is not pleasing to God for people to be deprived of this most vital form of personal kindness because His wishes are very much bound up with human fulfillment through physical love. The sexual drive in itself has no evil nature at all, no "original sin." Celibacy brings both men and women to great loss and suffering, exposing them to curiosity and ridicule and tempting them to irregularity in consequence. The rabbis say, "Do not talk to God and think of a woman; talk to a woman and think of God."

Marriage for non-Jews is performed by publicly acknowledging each other as spouses and then having sexual intercourse with the intent to consummate marriage. The couple are not married until both of these actions have been taken, and thus a man who is not capable of physical intercourse cannot reach the married state. There is even doubt as to whether a husband continues to be married if he loses the ability altogether. The wife assumes the family name of the husband according to universal custom, but even if this is not done the couple may be considered as married if they only live together openly with their names attached to the same residence. Most rabbinic opinions require written registration of marriage for the non-Jews as a way to validate the married status and to prevent adultery or incest occurring through misinformation. There is no need for any religious ceremony or sacrament, and the procedure known as "civil" or "registry office" marriage is quite sufficient. However, couples who are aware of the Seven Laws often accompany their marriages with ceremony suitable to the concepts.

The entry of the head of the male organ (glans) into the vagina is enough to constitute illicit relations. Anal penetration does not incur the penalty for adultery, but it does so for incest, for homosexual relations, and for bestiality. There is an opinion which states that marriage is consummated only by complete penetration of the male organ in the normal way, but this is not a ruling decision.

Divorce is the subject of rabbinic dispute because the Torah passage permitting divorce to the Jews ("and he shall write her a document of severance" [Deut 24:1]) can be interpreted in more than one way when applied to non-Jewish practice. One opinion maintains that because no divorce document is prescribed for the non-Jews, no divorce is ever possible. A second opinion holds that non-Jewish divorce is effected by verbal or other signs alone, on the initiative of either partner, with no document necessary. The third view is that since in Jewish law the man must divorce the woman, this alone is not possible for the non-Jews, and therefore only the woman can divorce the man. The second view has somewhat greater standing because it is subscribed to by Maimonides, the author of the most complete legal code of the Torah.

Without any clear preference between opinions on this subject, a community obedient to the Seven Laws may choose for itself the path by which it wishes to abide, and this will then constitute the obligatory law for that community.

A woman observer of the Seven Laws who marries should wear a covering on her hair as Jewish women do, according to the words of Proverbs 2:5, "The glory of God is to conceal a thing." However, if she becomes widowed or divorced, then unlike Jewish women she removes the covering and once more shows her hair, and this showing of the hair in public is one of the signs by which non-Jewish women effect the divorce itself.

According to the letter of the law, every man, whether Jew or Gentile, may have as many wives as he wishes. This is because a man is diversified by his nature, and a woman is integral; he may gather wives to his diversity, but she must have only one husband for her integrity.

Many societies have been based on polygamy, but there is not a single example in all the world of a society where women regularly have several husbands (polyandry) except in grossly distorted situations resulting from poverty or war. Thus the relationship of a married man with an unmarried woman is not adulterous but only extra-marital, though it is still a breach of personal trust. The harm to the individuals can also be very great because of the social ban preventing them from forming a marriage afterward without dissolving the existing family structure.

As generations go by, the human constitution becomes progressively weakened, so a thousand years ago it became "officially" impossible for a man to attend to the needs of more than one woman at the same time. It was decreed that Jews in western countries were forbidden to take more than one wife, while those of Oriental origin may still do so. Even Oriental life has declined in quality, and wives in polygamous families are much less well-situated than they were in earlier times. Western society has structured its life along the lines of monogamy so firmly that the prevailing custom has a strength close to law, something not to be treated lightly.

If a man undertakes the support of an extra wife, he must do so exactly as he supports the previous ones, and he must never force different women to share the same household and thus oppress each other or compete bitterly for his attention. He must give each one a household of her own, in a separate building, to be an undisturbed home for her and her children, and he must live with all in strict time rotation, so that no clash of interest ever occurs. Obviously, he can only attempt this if he has the money, but the preferred custom is for each wife to have a business or other earning activity of her own so that all are fully occupied with their maintenance and do not just wait idly for the husband, either personally or in money terms. It is also obligatory for all the wives to know of each other, without any deception or secrecy. The law as now given in Moslem countries is very similar to these principles.

Nevertheless, the basic law is that a man may take further wives without seeking the permission of those he already has. If he marries another woman supposing that his own wife is dead and she then reappears, he is in fact married to both of them. If a wife is insane or in a coma, she still has need of her husband's protection, and he need not divorce her in order to marry another. He may keep both of them at the same time. This is the normal Jewish practice today in such cases.

These laws often have to be applied in society, and they teach us much about the true nature of human love, providing solutions to many difficulties that come about through lack of reliable guidelines.

They provide one of the most important keys to understanding the real differences between men and women, which have become deeply obscured in today's world. An improvement in that understanding can only lead both men and women to greater happiness in each other's company.

Kings and other talented individuals throughout history, who have succeeded in living on a polygamous level, have been men whose capacities were great enough for them to match different wives to various aspects of their personalities. In former times it was thought necessary for a ruler to have many such relationships in order that his thoughts and ideas should increase in scope to cover the affairs of the nation.

However, it is certainly not required of anyone to strive for this level, and in general a man who multiplies his relations with the opposite sex is dissipating himself and wasting his capabilities. The conditions that must be fulfilled to maintain many wives in a happy and secure relationship are so stringent that only a tiny number of men can hope to meet them, however instructive the basic law may be.

The restriction against forbidden loves is an aspect of human life that has caused much resentment and confusion. People have always misunderstood the true intention of the restriction, but in recent times this misunderstanding has been encouraged. People need more than a vague advisory to make them ready to leave off a certain sexual relationship that they might otherwise enjoy. Modern secular life has made it an article of faith that love of all kinds is supreme, that nothing can be allowed to stand in the way of love, and that its result must always be good no matter what other people may say. Restraints on love relationships are considered old-fashioned forms of social repression that get in the way of personal fulfillment and that, because they cannot logically be proven beneficial, must be discarded altogether.

Yet it is this very same transcendent and heavenly nature of true interpersonal love that brings us back to the opposite conclusion. If people who love experience a union between themselves, which is also a union with God, then it follows that having physical love with those individuals whom God forbids to them will produce a relationship that is not as "heavenly" as they expect it to be.

A man who has relations with another's wife because her husband mistreats her is therefore not serving her interests as he should. A man who has become possessed of the desire for another man is not using his capacity for love on someone who should be receiving it. Love would hardly ever lead a person to desire intercourse with a horse or a dog, but whatever the motivation, acting out such a desire could only make a person less human, further out of touch with his or her own true nature.

When individuals begin to realize their personal need for an understanding of divine purposes, they will at that same time experience a development in their personal capacity for love. The realization that God is loving and not cruel, the gratitude for having been born and maintained alive and for the beauty of both the natural world and the moral law, will lead a person to regard Him in a loving way, to feel a wish to please Him and a reluctance to do anything that might give Him cause for pain.

With this realization comes the knowledge that human love is meant to be a reflection of the divine love, that if human beings relate to each other as God wishes then they also experience His love for them.

Thus they can moderate their desires and meet their human needs within the law: the wish to be known and understood by another person, to find favor even at times when they are at fault, to serve another's happiness with strength and passion, and to see the result in the form of children who will still be alive on the earth when they themselves must pass on.

Those who engage in forbidden relationships have no participation in all of this. Adulterous lovers may be very fond of each other, but their physical connection will not draw down upon them the divine pleasure that goes with true married expression. Homosexuals may experience all kinds of different sensations, but they will never transcend the level of regarding each other as objects, mere bodies which have no higher value.

This is because the law excludes a forbidden relationship from the power to transcend the limitations of the physical body, leaving the relationship flat and purposeless, unspiritual and "on the ground."

The rules of forbidden partnerships create boundaries for our lives, limits within which we can live happily but beyond which we run into trouble. Sometimes people cannot reconcile themselves to living within boundaries; they feel constricted, denied self-realization, and they treat the boundary rule as something invented to cramp their style.

In fact, it is only the soul of a person that is without limitations. The body is small and finite, with very little strength of its own, almost incapable of influencing the course of events without help from providential occurrences. If a person tries to transcend bodily limitations simply by using the body, he or she will surely feel the boundaries before much time goes by.

People may encounter limitations without knowing what they really mean. They can be convinced that the life of the body should not be limited, and they can set out to break the boundary rules that are there to help the expansion of the soul. In a society where the soul has been forgotten to the extent that it has in our own, the breaking of boundaries can reach the level where a new disease comes to the world. When a body becomes afflicted with AIDS, its own immune system breaks down, showing that the body's own boundaries can be vulnerable to the disregard of moral limitations. The AIDS epidemic, which has arrived in several forms out of the unknown, has for several years resisted all the efforts of science to find a purely medical cure. All the venereal diseases are similar warnings against careless sexual contacts, and their seriousness is evidence of how important it is to keep away from such things, modern drugs and prophylactics notwithstanding.

This is not to say that every relationship that is not forbidden by divine law will automatically be loving and kind. The sexual drive is strongly linked to harsh attributes such as egotism and jealousy, whose strength has to be diverted into loving ways before the relationship can be made to stand. It is only that the avoidance of forbidden relationships and practices is the key to realizing the link between our human love and the divine love; after that the relationship is ours to do with as we wish. If we put our heads and hearts into the relationship, then we will see a good result; if we neglect it for other reasons, then it will inevitably suffer.

A man's nature is to give and a woman's to receive. A man's nature is kindness and a woman's is strict judgment, the opposite of what many people are led to believe. It is because of the innate drive of strict judgment to link itself to kindness and thus restructure itself as kindness that a woman has such a strong desire to marry and have children. Her body is made to give milk, the epitome of kindness, but it cannot do so without the male contact.

Everything in the spiritual constitution of the world thus says that men and women must live together for this purpose, and that anything stemming from the forbidden loves is at cross-purposes with the basic intention.

And so the world is constructed in such a way that all the many forms of kindness and love, from giving donations to help refugees and famine victims or orphans to saying "bless you" when someone sneezes, have their root origin in obeying the rules that govern sexual love. We are born into the world through sexual relations, and they represent the most personal and intense form of love, the one which is our very "constitution," expressing our true individual outlook on life and on what we want to accomplish in it.

When we obey God's wishes regarding this essential basic love, we go to the source of ourselves and thereby realize our capacity to do truly loving things in every relationship, in everything we do. More than just by resisting the impulse to commit adultery when the temptation occurs, the gain comes through knowing that these laws exist, that they come from God and express His intentions for us, and that they are true and loving in and of themselves.

VIII

No rule of creation says that any individual is bound to break the sexual laws because of his or her own true nature. There is no such thing as "an adulterer" or "a homosexual" any more than there is such a thing as "a thief." All that exists is the temptation to wrongdoing that everyone experiences to some extent. Against this is only the need and desire of every person, Jew or non-Jew, to do as God wishes and to be respected and esteemed for it in His eyes.

The Torah refers to sexual immorality as "joking," a term that neatly explains the choice of the word "gay" as well as describing other forbidden relationships. Such relationships seem to be the most amusing way to pass the time, but in fact they make the participants into the "jokers" who place the joke squarely on themselves. By contrast it is the permitted and encouraged sexual relationship which provides real laughter. The couple laugh happily together in the knowledge that they are not doing anything shameful or contemptible.

The great majority of people who have sexual intercourse for the wrong reasons do so because they are depressed. Depression is an internalized form of anger, and in this case, the individual acts out his or her anger against external circumstances by seeking forbidden sexual pleasures. Soon the sense of humor becomes affected, and without even realizing it, the person turns this internal anger against God: "Why did He make me so deprived and unhappy? I'll break His rules and get someone else to do it with me, so then when He sees it He'll be sorry!"

Depression is so widespread today that many people do not even know that they are depressed. This is not surprising when the media, in their programs and advertising, cater to this way of life. When something is so widely considered legitimate, few people are going to assume anything is wrong with them.

Yet what brings happiness is the ability to refuse depressive sex and the other forms of consumption, including narcotic drugs which are so often a sexual substitute. We can realize that all things in this world that seem to be hostile or sad are in fact made to lead to good and that, in particular, we experience good directly when we refuse sexual immorality, even though such a refusal may seem a pointless loss when everyone else is apparently "having fun."

This is the working of the Sefirah of Kindness, the embrace of the "right arm." What seems to be a restriction has within it the power to bring us to true happiness.

Today, conventional psychological wisdom allows most people to retain their childhood antipathy to the "punishing parent" right on through adulthood; no one can tell them that the restrictions and the punishments might have had something valuable to say to them. They come to believe that what they want is good for them because they want it, without ever asking why it is that they want it, and this is one good way to become an unfulfilled individual.

Every person has the capacity to understand and follow the ideas explained here. The more one understands Torah and its reasons, the happier and more confident one will be, but the Creator gives the basic understanding to every human being.

Of all the forbidden relationships, incest with close relatives is the one that people most often consider disgusting and repugnant in and of itself. People seldom feel tempted to commit incest for reasons of ordinary sexual satisfaction or to further a friendship with the related person.

Even when incest does occur it is mostly an occasional thing, usually one time only; a stable sexual relationship between close relatives is something completely unknown. There is no movement to legitimize it, and no one goes out into the world saying openly that he or she is accustomed to practicing incest for personal fulfillment.

This is because the love feelings that exist between close relatives are of a completely different nature from those between sexual partners. The love of man and woman is intense and fiery; they long to be together and cannot bear to be apart. But a brother and sister have a cool, distant love; they are happy to be together, but their love is just as stable if they only meet rarely. It is this coolness that provides the reassuring factor in close family relationships, the knowledge that with the relative one can experience a love without passionate commitment or energetic effort.

When people decide to have incestuous relations, they deliberately go against a fact of nature that they know to be true, usually out of pure spite or sadism, and often, even more unhappily, without the other person's consent. Someone who reaches this level has lost contact with normal life in general, and though it can happen for a number of reasons, with severe depression among them, the rabbis say that a man who gorges himself sexually will come to "eat his own flesh," which means he will desire relations with his own flesh and blood. When sexual indulgence becomes an end in itself, the satisfaction within it is lost, and only the act itself in its most uncongenial forms appears as the lure.

Bestial relations are almost as revolting as incestuous relations to most people, but bestiality is more readily dismissed as laughable because no other person is involved and because of the ridiculous notion of setting up housekeeping with the dog. In crude or isolated company, a man may joke about the subject, but for a woman this is not nearly so easy, and few things can be so repellent as discovering that an acquaintance has extended his or her connections outside the species. These acts within more normal social settings stem from sexual overindulgence in general.

If a Jew has relations with an animal, then the animal must be killed by order of the court and its meat forbidden. The meat has a tainted status because it was a cause of sin, and people might come to look at it and to be tempted themselves, saying, "This is the animal which brought so-and-so to leave the path." If a non-Jew has relations with an animal, the animal need not be killed.

In striking contrast to the revulsion toward incest and bestiality, there is a widespread tendency to be lenient toward homosexual behavior and to vindicate the desire for homosexual relations. Millions of men and women set up households on such a basis, and though they are not considered examples of peaceful, healthy living by everyone, they often show a surprising stability. People leading such lives often hold responsible senior positions and make contributions to the arts or sciences. Books are written about the relationships themselves, which many praise for their high quality, and the allegedly superior "sensitivity" of this form of connection is constantly held up as a value worthy of universal adoption. Earlier societies also had homosexual elements, and they formed a key part of the workings of the society as a whole.

Why should something on this level be forbidden? The Seven Laws do indeed forbid homosexuality, on the same level as the other offenses just described, and no one can legislate any change to permit them. The Torah makes a particular point of forbidding homosexual marriage contracts to the extent that it praises those non-Jewish societies who refuse to register such marriages as upholders of the law.

Female homosexuality does not incur the penalty because women do not possess the physical means for intercourse, but sexual relations between women are termed "abominable" in the same way as male contacts without penetration and may not be tolerated.

What form of kindness is so missing in such relationships that the Almighty would set His face against them entirely? Even in times such as ours when the practice of homosexuality is widespread, large sections of society feel as much disgust for this practice as for incest and bestiality. Advocates of homosexuality try to portray its opponents as backward or ill-educated, but most ordinary people are not taken in. The establishment of homosexual municipalities that serve as a kind of "gay Camelot" and the wresting of concessions from city administrations evoke strong adverse reactions in many quarters even though people realize that little can be done about it for the time being.

At the opposite extreme of all this statuesque beauty is the reality unhymned by poets, the brutal and selfish homosexuality of both men and women seeking to enjoy the sexual attributes of each other in the most cynical and disillusioning way.

When people become aware of homosexual behavior in their midst, the revulsion they feel is against the improper use of kindness. Two men may feel that they want their capability for love to be used for each other, but the Seven Laws tell us that this is misplaced love. The beauty of a love relationship is only actualized when the love goes to its correct destination; otherwise it is like a letter sent to the wrong address, where one person ends up reading what is meant for another.

When love is misdirected in this way, the sexual partners never find their "address" in heaven. Their relationship remains empty of all the transcendence that correctly addressed love receives from above. Homosexual lovers become mere objects in each other's sight. They increasingly use each other, they become irritated and annoyed with small things, and the object of their affection starts to wear out and to lose its attraction. They place a premium on "fresh" relationships because the beauty of youth is all that can console the lovesick partner for the shortness of his time on earth.

Many have noted that the special poignancy so often felt by homosexual partners and described in their literature derives from an inner realization that they are indeed playing an "end-game"—their relationship goes no farther than themselves. A man and a woman gain by relating to each other sexually as objects, if their purpose is love, because the ultimate purpose of their relationship is to produce "another object," namely their child. Together they can set aside the limitations of personality and forget all its doubts and dissatisfactions. In these moments of intimacy, they receive the ultimate consolation for the transience of being in this world as a frail and perishable items, in the embrace designed by the blessed Creator, transcending it together with a partner who shares and understands that transience. But the homosexual participant never has children to live after him, nor does he enjoy a relationship that has its being in something eternal, something above the fading of his promise and the wrinkling of his skin.

Few men are more pathetic than the aging homosexual, uninteresting even to other homosexuals, abandoned to loneliness as the parade of new material passes him by. All the effort and trouble of married life and the raising of children is sound investment compared with the loss suffered by those who choose the "different way." In the end, all the societies that encourage homosexuality will likewise fade and decline.

Adultery with the wife of another man is not rare, but its contribution to unhappiness is as great as any single factor in love life. Depression and boredom, far more than genuine love for the woman, are responsible for the desire to abandon the home in secret and find transitory pleasure elsewhere. A husband who permits his wife to make other connections while remaining married to her does not exempt her from the adulterous designation; he is deliberately destroying his home rather than letting it be pulled down around him.

A husband's duty is to satisfy his wife so that their home provides all her needs because, without this, her natural tendency will be to stray outside its confines. He has to give her all her sexual requirements, without allowing her to become demanding, and give her the honor and respectability that allow her to go about in society with a good name. This maintaining of the home is the key to the stability and happiness in the religious sense that the Seven Laws recommend. In a certain way, the woman is herself the home; her body itself is like a home for the unborn child, and her position as the valued and respected center of all home life is an expression of her essential feminine nature, whatever other interests she might wish to pursue. Even the most able women, whose careers take them to the peak of success in the outside world, are reluctant to deny themselves this satisfaction altogether.

In modern life, few are aware of what a home really is or of how much a woman's life is downgraded by treating her sexual capacity carelessly and separating it from homemaking. Prostitution is one of the worst manifestations of this, and anyone who thinks that there is such a thing as a "happy hooker" should be straightened out. Even worse than prostitution, however, is the situation in which prostitutes are not needed because the good girls have been made to take over their function.

Pre-marital relations are harmful to the capacity for a healthy domestic life, but adultery destroys it altogether. If a man enters a bed that marriage has reserved to another, he is not just borrowing the facilities; he is wrecking the link between the man and the woman, for which their marriage is intended, and affecting their entire capacity for loyalty and trust. Their relationship can no longer exist as it did before.

When a woman has sexual relations with the man of her choice, she entrusts him with a deeply essential part of her nature. His sexual power is not something made to amuse her, only to be discarded like a toy; it conquers her and makes her part of a dual personality, the connection between two people which produces their children.

In Jewish marriage, this "acquisition" of the woman is the legal part of the ceremony. For this reason a Jewish woman cannot divorce her husband, though she can compel the court to make him divorce her. For non-Jews, this is not the case, and the man does not legally "acquire" the woman as a wife. However, the character of the arrangement is similar in the personal sense. A husband takes on the duty of maintaining his wife as the embodiment of his home, and she undertakes to perform that task in full integrity as long as they remain together.

Even though the law does not forbid the husband's outside connections as adultery, it is still deeply immoral for him to cheat on his life partner and go outside her realm for his gratification. She has the right to know where he is and how he spends his time and to go to him for household expenses and the needs of the children. Loyalty to one's spouse is like loyalty to God. When one passes over the other's faults because of the marriage tie that God has made, not seeking selfish pleasure or sulking when pleasure is not provided, then the faith and loyalty offer their own rewards in the form of understanding, enhancing every aspect of personal and family existence.

In order for a marital relationship to be successful, the partners must maintain their capacity for modesty and even for shame; they should not be afraid to blush. If something happens to disturb their opinion of each other, they should not have to take incident so seriously. The question has to be, "Am I so great anyway that I have to get annoyed over this?"

Blatant sexuality in the world has made it hard for people to remember the possibility of delicate feelings, of personal intimacy that occupies the private world inside and has no need to compete with what happens elsewhere. Modesty is not inadequacy; boundaries are not restrictions. If anyone asks the reason why, then the answer only has to be that there are laws for people's lives just as there are laws for the natural world: "Things are made to fall down, not up, and I'm doing as I was made to do."

This law corresponds to the blue color in the rainbow. Blue is the purest color and the closest to white, which represents original knowledge and truth. Blue is the color of the sky, a cool, soothing color, and it signifies the fulfillment of kindness and love, their peaceful nature which brings us near to heaven.

IX

While the prohibition of sexual misconduct is not always easily understood by the human mind, there is no such difficulty in understanding the reasons for forbidding murder. Most people, if asked what laws they would make in order to run the world properly, would immediately say that on no account must bloodshed of any illegal kind be allowed to go unpunished. Human life and personal safety are held by everyone to be the vital moral values, without which all life and happiness in this world would shrivel away to nothing.

Therefore we can appreciate how God Himself would never remain silent on the issue of murder. He would not leave the matter in human hands alone, without confirming in His laws how vital it is to protect human life. The second of the Sefirot, given the Hebrew name of *Gevurah*, which means "Strength," is the sign of His forbidding all wrongful use of might and power. Because God is the source of power, having by His power brought the world itself into being, His wish is that power be used to further His will alone. For this reason, the act of murder carries the death penalty by the hand of a sovereign court only, as the Torah states in the well-known passage, "Whoever sheds the blood of man, by man shall his blood be shed" (Gen 9:6). It is this passage, and not the injunction of the Ten Commandments ("You shall not murder"), that is the source of the law for non-Jews.

The passage from Genesis is a statement of law, not just a warning on what fate will befall a murderer. It is an instruction to the upholders of law to carry out the penalty because truth and integrity can only be maintained in this way. People might suppose that if one person has already been killed, then it serves no useful purpose to kill another. However, the law tells us that to leave a murderer alive in this way damages the whole world; the carrying out of the penalty is the only way to restore the balance and make restitution for what has been done.

Only one form of death penalty is permitted to the non-Jewish courts for their own people, and this is "beheading," the severing of the neck cord by one blow. This may be done by any means, such as a guillotine or even a bullet from a gun. The present-day method of hanging with the use of the "drop" is also valid because the death does not come through slow strangulation. Other forms of execution are more cruel, sometimes in subtle ways, and they do not accomplish the full spiritual reparation for the original crime. However, if a condemned person tries to escape, then he or she may be brought down and killed by any means rather than be allowed to remain at large.

The phrase "sheds the blood of man" refers only to the actual taking of life, not to wounding, even though this is also forbidden by the same passage. However, wounding does not incur the death penalty. Execution is the only permissible blood penalty. Inflicting scars or amputating limbs is not allowed for any offense. All woundings short of murder are to be repaid with monetary compensation alone. This scale of monetary payments for wounds is the only meaning of the Torah's phrase, "an eye for an eye" (Ex 21:29).

The law's protection is extended to the unborn as well as to the living. If the mother's life or life capacity is not in danger from the pregnancy, then no abortion may be carried out. The non-Jewish abortionist is to be tried in the same way as any other murderer. However, the mother's life may not be taken to save the child. An unborn child from forty days after conception differs from a living one only in its greater vulnerability, and removing it from the possibility of life is no different from "getting rid" of another inconvenient relative. Social pressures have increased to such an extent that many women are forced to obtain abortions against their better judgment, and their helplessness renders them victims of a general evil that sweeps love and decency ruthlessly out of its path.

A non-Jew is liable for ordering a killing and for taking life indirectly, as for instance by throwing a person into a pit and leaving them to starve or by exposing them to attack from a dangerous animal.

No one except the lawful government may give orders for war, and the cause for the war must itself be lawful. The only basic causes for military action are self-defense or the removal of potential state dangers including a threat to legitimate interests abroad, and the pre-emptive strike may be used to meet the emergency. However, there must be no crusade, no "holy war," no class war, no quest for glory in action, and no subjugation of races. This means the non-Jew cannot go to war, in the absence of a real threat to security, to conquer unbelievers in the name of the Seven Laws.

A defeated nation may resist the occupier if the occupation was unlawful—in the case of a naked attempt to conquer territory for gain, for example—but a lawful defeat must be accepted. If an unlawful conqueror succeeds in establishing rule in a way that the conquered people find acceptable, then armed resistance becomes illegal. In combat it is understood that there will be civilian casualties unless the battlefield is closely defined, but this must be kept to an absolute minimum. War atrocities, such as destroying villages in the line of march or killing prisoners as reprisals, are acts of murder punishable by the courts as in any other circumstances. A declaration of war does not turn a people into one single generalized target. The laws governing intelligence personnel and covert operations are different in their details, but they follow the same general outlines.

Persons who are near to death from wounds or disease may not have their lives shortened in any way, no matter how much pain and suffering they may be undergoing. Every moment of life on earth is precious because a person can only relate to God in a human way while alive in the body. The apparent "mercy" of easing the sufferer out of the world is in fact a greater loss than can ever be restored.

A person on the point of death may not be moved at all, even to make him or her more comfortable, because any movement at the time when the "flame of life" is flickering may cause it to go out altogether. Administering a pain-killing drug to the terminally ill is also likely to cause their hold on life to weaken. This prohibition applies in the case of a person about to meet death for a reason other than illness. For example, if a person is teetering on the edge of a cliff, one may not put that person to death in a more "preferable" way.

Because our bodies were created by God and not by ourselves, we are not allowed to kill ourselves, and suicide is classed as murder. No one may aid another to commit suicide or encourage a person to do so for whatever reason. States that have recently begun furnishing suicide materials to elderly people on a contingency basis are committing a most serious crime. The concept that people who are in pain, or who are useless, or who are burdensome to society are candidates for suicide is part of the abuse that has crept into society through mechanization. These are among the most inhuman and unspiritual suggestions in all existence, completely opposed to God and His love. However, suicides who are not deliberate in their action are not considered liable in any religious way, and they are not treated differently from any other person dying of natural causes.

There is no place of sanctuary to which murderers can escape, nor is there any ransom payable to release them from the penalty. Non-Jews must refuse to commit murder, even when threatened with their own deaths. However, they may break any of the other Seven Laws to preserve their own lives.

A non-Jew who does not observe the Seven Laws (a heathen) is liable to the death penalty for killing another non-Jew through negligence, and people should never expose themselves or others to dangerous risks for no good reason.

The wasting of male seed through masturbation is not a sexual offense but is in the same category as murder. The seed is the life substance of the man and contains the potential for creating other human beings, and therefore it has a high value and must not be emitted in vain, whether by himself or during a sexual act with another. A woman's masturbation does not have the same high value because there is no emission, but it is also called "wasting seed" and should not be done. Like the sexual offenses, this tends to happen mostly in circumstances of depression, and there is likewise a vicious cycle where the act committed to escape depression becomes a further cause of it. This need never prevent anyone from coming to a true realization and avoiding the problem. There is no court punishment for vain release or masturbation, and there is no prohibition on sexual relations with a woman who is unable to have children.

All these safeguards show clearly how great is the value assigned to human life and how abhorrent is any tendency to waste or cheapen it.

Even people who do not cherish the lives of others seldom kill with complete wantonness. Anyone who takes life has a reason for doing so in his or her own mind, even the Nazi who classifies the Pole or the Jew as "subhuman" or the American gangster who "plugs" someone for "crossing the gang."

But the Seven Laws require us to take this basic realization to a far higher level, to regard human life as the most precious deposit we have in our hands, and to never take it without specific legal sanction no matter what other gain might come from doing so.

The aspect of strength and power in this law connects it to the red color in the rainbow, the color of blood, and the sign of fierce power on all flags and emblems. This is the hottest color, used to signify fear or danger in emergency situations, concerning fire or other urgent peril which needs no other explanation and leaves no place for equivocation.

X

Human ownership of property was present in the world from the moment of the creation of the first people. Adam and Eve were told that all the world with its living things belonged to them to use as they wished, and this first right of property was later divided between the different nations who descended from Noah. However, they were also told that one thing only was not in their hands to use, and this was the "tree of knowledge of good and evil" that stood in the middle of the Garden of Eden. God told him and his wife, "You shall not eat of it, for in the day that you eat of it you shall surely die" (Gen 2:17). When they disobeyed and ate its fruit, they committed the offense of using property that was not theirs, the root of the act of stealing.

The different interpretations of what this Tree of Knowledge signified, what kind of tree it was, and what were the effects on the man and woman when they ate its fruit come down only to the basic fact that it had been forbidden to them. It was not a drug or a poison that made them die, nor was it even a "forbidden fruit" that had the power in itself to cause them moral harm. The only thing that made them wrongdoers was that they took something that did not belong to them, something that had been placed by God in another ownership, namely in His alone.

This principle still applies today to all property that is legally in the hands of another person, not only to holy things reserved for God.

It was in His hand to give us the right of ownership for ourselves because He is the owner and master of all that He created. Therefore, when we own our movables and our land we become like Him, close to Him in His attribute of mastery. Thus, it is our ownership that gives us the power to act in a Godly way toward others. Only when we own property can we be generous and kind with it. Might and power, with which we gain our holdings and defend them, also gives us the ability to use what we have to help and support ourselves and others. The combination of the first two Sefirot, Kindness and Strength, creates the third Sefirah, which is known as *Tiferet* or "Beauty" and corresponds to the human torso with its many organs functioning together in harmony. The root of all such harmony is our own honesty, and so this Sefirah represents the positive values that stand opposite all acts of stealing, cheating, and kidnapping.

The law of the Ten Commandments, "You shall not steal," does not prohibit either Jew or non-Jew from stealing property but only forbids the Jew from kidnapping another Jew and using him as a slave, which incurs the death penalty. If a Jew abducts another Jew into his own hands and uses him as a slave in any way, however small, and then sells him to anyone else, the Jewish court renders him liable to execution, as the rabbinic explanation of the passage specifies. A Jew is liable as a thief for kidnapping a non-Jew. The Jewish prohibition against stealing property is found in Leviticus 19:11, "You shall not steal, nor deal falsely...." This section is also the source of many other commandments to the Jews concerning wrongful transaction.

The prohibition against theft is among the seven principal laws because theft is an offense against the divine will itself, not just a private matter for a wronged individual to settle on his or her own. When Adam and Eve ate the fruit wrongfully, they lost their ability to live forever and became liable to die, as all of us today still do. This happened because they disturbed the moral order that God created for them and entrusted to them to maintain. We too are given this order of beauty to safeguard for ourselves, and we know all too well how much damage is done to it by ordinary crime, by casual neglect of the sanctity of what belongs to others, and by systematic attempts to tamper with ownership (such as those of the Communist movement).

Non-Jews are liable for theft no matter what the value of the articles they steal, but Jews are not liable unless they steal something of a certain minimum value, about three American cents in current terms. However, stealing something worth less than the minimum for liability is still forbidden to the Jew. The non-Jew is liable for withholding due wages, for impounding an article deposited with him, for looting in wartime, and for kidnapping any other person, all whether secretly or openly. Jews are forbidden all these acts under separate headings, but for the non-Jew the single law of theft covers them all.

The rape of a woman is an act of theft, not a sexual misdemeanor, and as such it incurs the full liability from the court. Stealing from another thief is still considered stealing. A Jew is liable for theft from a non-Jew, and so also a non-Jew from a Jew, each under the laws that pertain to themselves.

The laws of property transactions vary from place to place, but their purpose is always to ensure that people have effective ownership of the assets they possess. Trade and business exist because the world is made in such a way that things are produced far away from the places where they are needed. The processes of gathering materials, manufacturing goods, and distributing those goods carries the whole world from its original state to the one it will have when it reaches its destiny. This is accomplished by means of money, which is a medium specifically designed and standardized for outgoings. When this is done in full legality and trust, the destiny of all humanity is brought closer because the honest nature of the transactions fulfills God's true intention.

Jews may not pay each other interest on loans, but non-Jews may pay interest to each other. Both Jews and non-Jews may pay interest on money borrowed from the other. During the Middle Ages, the Christian and Moslem religions took this prohibition against charging interest, intended to apply only to Jews, and applied it to their own peoples. There was no true Torah basis for this practice, and it only maintained the rigid and unjust feudal system by rendering wealth static and unconvertible. The practice distorted financial matters and gave non-Jewish interest transactions a stigma that did not belong to them. The task of credit management in the economy was assigned solely to the Jews, who, at the same time, were accused of systematic violation of the rights of property, an indication of the cynical turn of the Exile at this stage. When non-Jews began modern banking at the time of the Reformation, they removed this great psychological stumbling-block and restored the issue of charging interest to non-Jews to its true status under the Seven Laws.

In today's world, there are only two forms of property, namely movables and land, with the money value through which they are assessed and transferred. In former times there was also slave property, the holding of individuals in an unfree situation for economic purposes. The question of the enslavement of people by others has caused enormous agitation and heartache in the past, and its after-effects continue to do so. This has happened because of misunderstandings about the attribute of mastery and the ways in which men and women become master over one another.

A non-Jew who enslaves another can never acquire that individual's actual body as property. All the master can gain is the product of the enslaved person's labor. The master never acquires any personal rights in the slave, such as affection or allegiance, and certainly no sexual privileges whatever. The master may not work the slave to the extent of harming his or her health or causing physical injury. Anyone who kills a slave becomes liable to the death penalty. Any other claims are illegal according to the law of the Torah.

Slavery has been known in all societies of the world, European, Indian, Chinese and African, from ancient times until very recently, and it would probably be true to say that most of humanity, of all races and colors, are the descendants of slaves from one time or another. The Jews themselves were enslaved in Egypt for hundreds of years before they were brought out by the divine hand. Nevertheless, there is no obligation in the Seven Laws to enslave anyone or to hold slaves. Even though the Torah speaks of the descendants of Ham, the youngest son of Noah, as being "a slave to his brethren," this does not mean that they have to be enslaved or cannot live as free persons like all others.

In essence non-Jewish individuals may only become enslaved if they sell themselves into slavery, being presumably in urgent need of money, or if their king decrees that they be sold as a slave in punishment for some offense against the royal jurisdiction. The slavery may be for life or for a certain period only, like that of the indentured men who came from England to work in colonial America for a limited time without free movement or pay. A Jewish man may have slavery decreed on him by the Jewish court or may sell himself into slavery, but he may only be enslaved to a Jewish master under specified terms, and if he is sold to a non-Jew then he must be bought out again. A Jewish woman never becomes enslaved under this law, nor does a convert to Judaism.

In addition to this, a Jewish or non-Jewish king who captures prisoners in the course of a war may dispose of them as slaves. There is doubt about whether a private person, in the absence of government authority, may enslave others simply by capturing them. This would usually be considered ordinary kidnapping because individuals cannot set themselves up as rulers to do what they wish even when there is no government authority. The general understanding is that no conqueror may enslave an entire population, as the Nazis attempted to do in several countries. A private person who abducts the slaves of another and assumes mastery over them is guilty of stealing. Non-Jewish children are born as slaves if that is the status of their fathers but not of their mothers. If the mother is a slave but the father is not, the child is born as a free person.

It is forbidden for non-Jewish kings to make war simply in order to capture slaves, just as it is forbidden to them to undertake the conquest of lands held by others. However, if they do so, then the lands and the persons they capture become theirs.

Lands in general do not become the property of the peoples who live in them unless a formal legal claim is made. In the case of peoples such as the North American Indians and the Australian Aborigines, who lived without the concept of overall property, there is considerable doubt as to whether they ever properly claimed the land. Therefore, the law presumes that it was the Europeans who made the first true claims on these lands and that consequently the lands belong entirely to them. Of course, this gives no reason at all for the original inhabitants to be enslaved or mistreated in any way.

Enslaved persons become free if they buy themselves out from under the slavery, if the master frees them for any reason, and if the king or other sovereign authority decrees that any or all of the slaves are to be freed or that slaveholding is to be abolished. Those who become free are in exactly the same position as any other individuals in society, with no trace remaining of their former status. According to the law, slaves who escape do not become free until their masters give up the attempt to reclaim them. However, there have always been special places of sanctuary from which escaped slaves could not be reclaimed, and crossing the border into a non-slave-holding territory is an equivalent to crossing into a sanctuary. Enslaved non-Jews remain bound by the Seven Laws but cannot become fully converted to Judaism until they are freed. By the law of the Torah an escapee who reaches the land of Israel is considered free and becomes a full convert on declaring his arrival.

Because property and ownership are related to mastery, kindness is easily forgotten, and the impulse to gain land and goods at any cost is strong. People have an "evil inclination," and they can easily convince themselves that something they see and want is for that reason something they should have. Thus, they come to believe that it is theirs in actuality, and they can soon take it with only a little misgiving about who really is entitled to it.

Most people are not criminals in the sense that they deliberately take money or articles that they know belong to others, but when ownership is doubtful or the means of acquisition is only slightly unethical, then it is only too easy to set qualms aside and "go for it" with an untroubled mind. The business environment encourages actions like these, terming them "initiative" or "enterprise," and it is true that the world of business and trade would never function if people were not acquisitive or dynamic in pursuing wealth and gain. The Zohar comments on the first section of the Book of Genesis, "A man's good inclination was created for himself, and his evil inclination for the sake of his wife"—to seek out and bring home all the material things she needs.

However, a man who knows how the Torah regards theft even in these concealed ways will be able to provide for all his needs without infringing on forbidden territory even in the slightest instance. The evil inclination can be happy doing its work of sustaining the family without any need to shaft competitors unethically, to overcharge vulnerable customers, to make dubious claims for the product, to divert funds without telling the owner in order to cover a temporary loss, or to take home a side profit before declaring it to one's partner. The urge to permit these practices may be extremely strong, but the man of enlightenment will realize that they are all false and that complete honesty is the only way to travel.

This approach does not stem merely from fear of the police. For success in this regard, one must realize that God Himself sees everything, that He takes interest in whatever each individual does, and that the reckoning is not delivered to the boss or even to the wife but to His judgment alone. This approach also requires that one not see material things as valuable in themselves but rather that one should "dilute" materialism until its true value comes through. Business then becomes a vehicle for honesty as an end in itself, with moral satisfaction to bring home at the end of the day, and profits become a means to live in comfort and to provide for all legitimate needs.

Stealing affects the personality in a way that would discourage anyone who understood this from doing the deed. Habitual criminals become crude and degraded in their habits and appearance, losing out heavily on all forms of true happiness and love. The worst gangsters are men with nothing left of their human aspect, the "image of God." Their leadership is uncouth and clumsy, without any of the distinction shown by a successful businessperson, let alone a king. They have no honor, no statesmanship, no poetry, no love of life, nothing except money and all the sleazy ways they can think of to get hold of it. Only naive or slavish people have any desire for their company, far less any wish to marry or care for them, because they lose the ability to attract a reputable person. The lesser forms of theft come to tempt everyone, and petty thievery offers all these ill effects in smaller and less obvious forms.

Business morality is at the top of the agenda today for Jews and non-Jews alike. The harshness of workplace and marketplace is something that everyone feels, and the world now knows that nothing can be done about it by changing property ownership itself, still less by trying to abolish it altogether. However, the morality of the Seven Laws, as expressed in the intention of the commandment forbidding theft in all its forms, has the capacity to set the business world on its feet and to give it the dimension of beauty that it now lacks. No other moral system has ever succeeded in doing this, and it cannot be effective unless in harmony with the Jewish commandments themselves. This is possible only now because the world has come to the point where Jews and non-Jews work together in the economy.

The most important of the Jewish commandments concerning business is not to engage in it on the Sabbath. If this is respected, then all the business activities of the weekdays become elevated and sanctified, and this makes room for the observance of the precepts dealing with unfair gain.

Non-Jews are not commanded to observe the Sabbath, but all the provisions that they make in their economy to enable the Jews to observe it open the door to safeguarding themselves from theft and redeeming their own businesses from harsh ways. By these means the world's workings may come to true harmony, without protectionism, job discrimination, or environmental carelessness, moving smoothly and in prosperity toward the redemption that will relieve us from our toil.

The aspect of beauty enhanced by the keeping of this commandment links it to the yellow color of the rainbow. This is the color of the sun, the source of all beauty and a metaphor for happiness and joy. It signifies complete freedom from distress or worry, a scene of confidence where the world is a delightful place, as it was meant to be.

XI

The first three Sefirot are concerned with the relationships we ourselves form with each other, and they relate to God only through showing the interest that He takes in our situation and the reasons why He commands us as He does. However, the next two Sefirot in the sequence, the pair known as *Netzach* (Eternity) and *Hod* (Glory), show our direct connection with Him, as can be seen from their more abstract, elevated names. This brings us into the area understood more directly as "religion": the knowledge of God, the love and awe of Him, and the concepts surrounding His worship and service.

If it were not for the fact that God Himself has commanded that only He may be worshiped, one might be entitled to suppose that, even if He is the only Creator, He has given permission to people to worship anything they choose, just as they choose their own personal friends or decide whatever they like to eat. If this were so, no harm would come from any form of idolatry, any selecting of things to venerate.

However, His instruction to the non-Jew to worship Him alone is stated in Genesis 2:16, "And the Lord God commanded it upon the man [Adam], saying...." The word "commanded" means that He as the source of all commands is the only God to be served. The rabbis give the interpretation that this even prohibits a worshiper from serving another entity along with the actual Creator, this being known as "partnering." The law against idolatry thus affirms God's rulership over all of His creation, as expressed in the Sefirah of Eternity.

Likewise, the commandment against blasphemy, which is the use of God's name for cursing, affirms His love for everything that He made. When observed, this commandment activates our thanks to God, and this corresponds to the Sefirah of Glory. The Torah states this commandment in Leviticus 24:16 and specifically includes the non-Jew: "And he who utters the Name of the Lord blasphemously...both the stranger and the resident...." These two commandments operate as a pair, like the legs that support the body, the only two of the Sefirot that always do so, and it is an essential truth of religion that God's love and His rulership are never separated but go together at all places and times.

History tells us of a great mistake made by the early generations before Noah. People began to assume that the heavens had been created by God to serve as His attendants, showing by their lofty status how He in turn was immeasurably lofty, and that therefore it would please Him if the heavens were to be honored and worshiped as beings close to Him. They did not imagine that these created things were gods; they knew the one Creator had made them all, but their mistake lay in assuming that by serving His creations they would fulfill His will.

Later they fell under the influence of false prophets who spoke in the name of stars or angels, and they began to pay direct homage to created entities. First they sought intercession with God by asking the heavenly bodies, the stars, moon and sun, and then they ascribed beneficent powers to the bodies themselves. Soon also they did this with earthly items such as mountains, trees, and animals. Finally, they erected their own creations specially designed for worship.

This went on until all humanity, for most of historic times, was organized into cults of veneration. Each national or tribal group expressed its collective personality by choosing an object that it felt was most powerful and closest to its nature. Archaeologists never conduct an investigation without finding items of wood, metal, or stone that either were worshiped in themselves or were meant to represent some more abstract element of worship, such as the fertility of the ground or the power of wind and thunder.

The forms of worship in those days were not generally of an uplifting kind. Sacrifices were cruelly performed, sometimes on human beings. Drunkenness and sexual exploitation were common, and priests used their power to justify heavy taxation and deceptive practices in order to enhance their own privileged position. Tribes waged war under the protection of the ruling object and sometimes ostensibly by its actual command to subdue the adherents of rival cults and take their lands or property. In those early times, idol worship showed how moral damage can come from not recognizing the true religious path. The term "freedom of religion" does not mean simply the right to worship anything that one likes or "idolizes." If people yield to their natural impulse to deny their Creator in favor of an easier veneration of idols, they lose contact with His love, and then any atrocious conduct can be justified.

People in our own generation are no longer so stupid as to ascribe divine powers to objects selected by them or made by their own hands. But in a more subtle way, the idolizing tendency is still very much with us. Money and the power it brings are often elevated to a near-divine status. The "stars" of show business, of politics, and of sports are placed among the higher beings whose influence is considered radiant and benign. People are encouraged to venerate the human form, human relationships (especially with their love partners), and often even love itself. The sciences, especially sociology and psychology with their promise of control over the human mind, have achieved the final irony by making rationality into a cult of its own, complete with priests, servers, and faithful followers who will hear nothing of any other idea.

The tendency even today is to regard venerated beings as possessing the right to decide which conduct is moral. When such thinking is challenged, the usual answer is that people have a "religious impulse" that should be satisfied by whatever candidate they find nearest or most convenient. This is called "freedom of religion," but usually it produces a confused situation where shortcomings are universal and reliable truths are hard to find. In a society that knows nothing of the Seven Laws, people could be forgiven for thinking that this is a situation in which the Almighty Himself has placed them.

The major non-Jewish religions of today are not in the same class as the idolatrous faiths of ancient times in this respect. The major religions have diluted the crudity of the ancient practices and introduced some true ideas from the Jewish sources, producing an admixture designed to appeal both to idolatrous tendencies and to the desire for genuine truth. The Moslem faith has received the best interpretation, as its ordinary worshiper is considered to be praying to the Creator Himself without any interposition. Nevertheless, Moslem doctrines, especially those concerning the Mecca site with its "black stone," are not free from idolatrous content. Moreover, Islam does not practice its faith in the name of the Torah. Christianity is more deeply implicated in idolatry, based as it is on establishing Jesus as an extension of the divinity and thus as an intermediary for both belief and prayer. The Jewish people do not offer one of their number for this purpose or anything similar to it.

Though Buddhist and Hindu practices today proclaim belief in an overall Creator, unlike their early forms of expression, their idolatrous nature is still marked, and their philosophies are subject to error in consequence. Cultic faiths that have developed from eastern origins in recent years are so far from purity as hardly to deserve description.

All through the liturgy and customs of these religions can be found traces of the idolatries of former times. One of the most prominent of these is the *asherah*, the sacred grove of trees that survives today in the form of the Christmas tree. Ancient fertility rites are still commemorated by the Easter egg, and the Easter Bunny has its origin in worship of female powers associated with the springtime. These practices are not as reprehensible as the early idolatries themselves, but the non-Jew who learns of the Seven Laws and whose mind begins to improve along their pathways will feel reluctant to put gifts under a tree erected in his or her house at the midwinter time. The appearance of serving a false deity will be enough for him to give presents to his loved ones in a different way and to spend the season in other less compromising activities.

Priestly and monastic practices are common to all these non-Jewish faiths, and their distinctive feature is an unnatural mode of life, without normal family relations or social interaction. Truth does not demand that individuals set themselves apart in this way. Such practices as celibacy have very little to teach people, and it is well known that the members of such orders are subjected to great personal strain and temptations of the worst possible kind.

Much of the trouble comes from the reliance of these religions on an intermediary who stands between the human beings and their Creator. There is an insistence that non-Jews need and want this "partnership" in their worship. The ecumenical movement even promotes a loosely organized "world idolatry" in which one is free to choose one's particular "partnership element" on a local or personal basis.

The Torah indicates that this is not a true need for non-Jews, however strongly it may be felt, and that behind the similarity of all world religions lies a deeper unity, the true non-Jewish nature to which the Seven Laws correspond. One Creator made all human beings, and they descend from a single ancestor. No one can claim superiority over another on the basis of his or her ultimate origin, and the man in whom that origin lies would not have merited to become the father of so many different peoples unless he had rejected all such religious admixtures entirely. His merit came from pure devotion to God as the one Ruler, and God repaid his loyalty by saving his life and establishing his truth for ever.

XII

The feeling of uprightness and dignity that comes to the non-Jew who sets his or her face against the practices discussed in previous chapters is still so rare that few people can even imagine what it would be like. They may from time to time have doubts about the level of intelligence behind the prevailing customs, but social pressures are so strong that without actual knowledge of the Seven Laws hardly anyone can go further.

Yet doubts about the customs of his time led Aimé Pallière to find what he needed. He felt the need to make a social leap, and Rabbi Benamozeg reassured him that inside every non-Jew, no matter what appearance the accretions of false faith might give, was a person whose need and desire was only for these commandments, simply because they were given by the same God who created him. For the rest of his life Pallière felt a greater closeness to his fellow non-Jews because he had gained an understanding of what they really were.

Many non-Jews feel that their natural inclination is to experience divinity through intermediaries. They see the wondrous powers of nature and find life and beauty.

They investigate creation through scientific methods and discover untold wisdom and complexity, and it all speaks to them of one thing: the glory of God as He chooses to manifest it.

Yet for all the lessons in these experiences, their true significance does not become clear unless they are placed in the context of the direct word of God to humanity, namely the moral law, the Seven Commandments. For just as humanity is placed above nature, so human morality is above natural laws. When God wishes to give us an important instruction, He speaks to us directly, through His chosen prophets such as Moses. When He wishes us to infer something less important from the workings of the world, He allows us to discover it for ourselves.

Therefore the primary experience of the divine cannot come through any intermediary means, such as the Jesus figure or the Buddhist tutelaries or nature as either science or art conceives it. They are very different from the prophets who raised themselves to holy levels to be worthy of receiving divine revelations. Even at those high levels, the prophets remained men like all others, with no divine status of their own apart from what their knowledge of holy Torah had given them. Only the human moral stature, achieved through obedience to the divine will, can claim to raise either the individual or the group to a level of union with truth. Once people arrive at this level, all their other activities gain a new life and significance. Their art and science no longer suffer from carrying burdens of invalid meaning but become free to search for true beauty and valid expression. Now, in our own time, many more people are coming to learn about the Seven Laws and to experience them for themselves because it is not enough merely to become aware of

God's existence. Once He is found, the obvious next step is to ask what are His wishes and intentions. The generation preceding our own was threatened with great moral imbalance in the form of deviant cults such as the Nazis and Communists and their various sympathizers. The damage the Nazis did to human life and property, as well as to dignity and truth, was so great that even three generations after their defeat in a terrible war the world has not fully appreciated the cost.

The hostility of these movements to religious morality went beyond the regular human consciousness of the times. They invoked pagan ideas that had lain dormant since early times, proving that such ideas had not gone out of existence altogether. Nazism derived from the sins of the generation before the flood, a generation that incorporated murder and violent robbery into the state itself. Communism relates to the generation of the Tower of Babel, a generation that conscripted labor brigades for a building project and disrupted family life with false teachings. Therefore, Nazism was defeated in chaos and catastrophe, whereas Communism melted and dispersed quietly.

In order to commit their outrages, they had to establish ruling cults in which their ideas were worshiped and the men who embodied those ideas became objects of veneration. By thus dethroning morality as it derives from Godly sources, they were able to perpetrate the destruction with which all the world is now familiar.

The Jewish people have been the prime target of all such movements throughout history, ever since Abraham himself challenged King Nimrod. The Nazis and Communists, as well as the Arab nationalists, understood that they would never succeed as long as the Jewish religion was freely allowed. The non-Jewish nations of the world also suffered in their deepest moral nature, their true happiness and prosperity, from these "enemy occupations." They fought against them with dedication, and their victory was a victory for freedom in the widest sense of the term.

The element that such evil movements had in common was that of exploitation. They deceived people and stole their sense of truth, replacing it with hysterical states of mind which prevented regular life as happy people know it. All forms of idolatry deprive people of their right to relate to God in a pure, unimpeded way, offering only false gratifications in return.

The defeat of Nazism and Communism through the efforts of the United States and its allies has now given the final go-ahead to the revelation of the true ideas of religious freedom for which those countries stand. Since America has become the main home for the Jewish people and their Torah under free conditions, nothing stands in the way of America's duty to give its non-Jewish neighbors the fruit of the long effort to uproot dangerous ideologies from the world. The State of Israel, with its American connection, represents the Jewish national identity as it applies directly to public affairs, and it too has been fighting the tyrannies of the spirit as manifested in pan-Arab nationalism.

People who cannot bear to live under the rule of Adolf Hitler, Joseph Stalin, or Saddam Hussein have the right to learn about the Torah that those dictators tried to destroy. The commandment of Torah that forbids idolatry to the non-Jews also urges them both to repent and to pray, to make their contribution to spiritual well being in general. In this way the rabbis derive many other statutes that guide and inform non-Jews in their relationship with God. After pursuing the desire to relate to God in a religious way, the individual returns to his or her own world with more and better information on how to establish moral security, ready to cope with challenges and achieve satisfaction.

God Himself is the only ruler, and yet He also created our world that contains misrule and immorality. Therefore, the human task, for both Jew and non-Jew with their different approaches, is to avoid being deceived into believing that God created immorality in order to allow it. The divine intention is that people should recognize God alone and turn from the falsehoods which He has permitted so that the merit of the correct choice will elevate human beings and thus establish His kingdom in the world through them alone.

God allows false worship even though He does not desire it because He is above the mistakes of humankind. As the rabbis expressed it, "Why should He destroy His world for the sake of fools?" Because of His love for humanity, He has patience with their follies and waits until they will see the truth for themselves.

Jewish writings appeal primarily to the intelligence and to the logical faculty in particular. There is no arbitrary doctrine to confuse the mind, no demand that reason be set aside to serve higher purposes.

Discussions of truth are most often discussions of law. One must be a legalist, not in the sense that one takes a narrow view of oneself or others, but in the sense that one is willing to debate different views and, on the basis of the outcome, to take on an obligation.

The legal element in Jewish life is comparatively well-known, but the existence of the Seven Laws for all non-Jews is far less appreciated. The possibility that non-Jews can live a life exactly suited to their non-Jewish nature yet have all the advantages of Jewish thought comes as a surprise to most people. To be told that the religions to which they are accustomed are still against the spirit of a divine edict may raise questions in their minds, but those questions can be answered with complete respect for the person and the intelligence.

All the Seven Laws are expansive categories, and the prohibition against idolatry brings into its scope all the ways in which religious life may come to error. Superstitious beliefs such as astrology or palmistry take people away from the true path; even though such practices may tell us something about future events, they cannot tell us everything. Those who direct their actions based on superstitious beliefs are bound to go astray. Divination through spirits, like communication with the souls of the departed, is a quasi-idolatrous practice. Although the rabbis dispute whether such practices incur the full penalty for idolatry, they agree that they make no contribution to personal advancement or stability.

Non-Jewish individuals who observe this commandment have a religious life of direct contact with divinity. They relate to God in truth when their lips move in prayer, whether alone or in a group, because their knowledge of Torah helps them to pray accurately and intelligently, without being sidetracked into topics for which they have no real need. Any individual can gain all the knowledge that he or she needs to realize the true self and relate it to its source on high. No one is ever denied this if one wants to find it. All through human history, people have experienced moments of true prayer in this way when their situation demanded it, with all the surface accretions of false religion suddenly forgotten; knowledge of the Seven Laws can enable them to live like this all the time.

Some of the Jewish festivals are relevant to observers of the Seven Laws. The two days of Rosh Hashanah, the Jewish New Year, represent the annual renewal of the world when God assesses all human beings in judgment. Non-Jews may not mark the occasion in the same way as Jews, namely by abstaining from work or performing the other commemorative ceremonies, but if they are conscious of the significance of the day, directing their thoughts in accordance with its meaning, then they fulfill their part in it. The Shavuot festival, the anniversary of the giving of the Torah, is important for non-Jews because the Seven Laws were given at that time also.

Non-Jews may celebrate their own birthdays (on the Hebrew calendar) in a religious way, and they can join in the general holidays of their nations, such as the Fourth of July in the United States.

The minor Jewish holidays are special times for all humanity because of the good news associated with them. Chanukah in particular commemorates the defeat of those arrogant non-Jews who tried to abolish both the Jewish Torah and the Seven Laws that applied to themselves.

However, non-Jews must not keep the Jewish Sabbath or the other festivals specific to Jews, wear the *tefillin* on the head or arm, fix a *mezuzah* with Torah writings on the household doorpost, or be called to a public reading of the Torah. Nor may non-Jews write these articles, as a Jewish scribe would do. Non-Jews may not make a new religion or invent religious events for themselves, not even based on the Seven Laws, such as a remembrance of the end of the flood. Most male observers of the Seven Laws do not wear any special covering on their heads as Jewish men must do, so as to avoid being mistakenly identified as Jews.

XIII

The existence of afterlife for all humanity is an unchallengeable fact, something that every person knows instinctively from the very nature of his or her creation. The reward of following the Seven Laws can be felt in this world, but the full reward is given only in the next. This world is the place for effort, for which we are given physical bodies as well as human intellect and emotions to move them, and anything that requires effort must necessarily be limited in duration.

The next world is the place of souls, which know no eating and drinking or having children but only the radiance of the divine Presence, each according to his or her achievements here and now. There the falsehood of idolatry is fully exposed, with no deceptive appearances such as exist on earth to disguise reality. One Creator made us all, both the Jews and the "righteous of the nations," and He alone has the power to give us our reward when we come before Him to be questioned on our deeds. The way in which these benefits are acquired is through the study of the Torah. When we know God through the writings that He has given to us through His prophets, then we have no trouble deciding how to approach Him or knowing what will be pleasing to Him. Non-Jews may not study those parts of the Torah that are not relevant to the Seven Laws, but all of the twenty-four books of the Scriptures bring them to knowledge of God, as do the later rabbinic works that enhance their capacities for understanding. The Talmud and its commentaries are filled with references to the Seven Laws and the relationships derived from them, and so there is no shortage of topics for inquiry even after the portions concerning Jewish matters are excluded.

Present-day non-Jewish religions have a place for people who want morality and Godliness, but these religions lack the capacity to satisfy that need. They have contradictions that they disguise as "life's mystery" or shortcomings that they dismiss as "human failing." People have to earn a living and carry on their personal lives as well as maintain their religious affiliation, and most people lack the time or the energy to question structures that have endured for so long; it is usually enough that at least somebody cares and that something plausible is on offer.

In addition, there are uncounted millions throughout the world whose connection with organized morality is very loose or who have no religious commitment at all. Often they can see through the inadequacy of today's religions with their history of falsehood and war. They have their basic human goodness to carry them through life, but they suffer from the lack of any path for development along moral lines.

These shortcomings are inescapable as long as non-Jews remain restricted to religions that damage the divine rulership or to no religion at all. The early Christians who protested to their "Godfearer" friends that human nature could not bear the real truth and so must be given an outlet for its desire to idolize were completely mistaken. The centuries of Christian ideological rule that followed were so filled with harshness, insincerity, and sheer confusion that their original monopolistic claims have not survived into the present time. The American and the French Revolutions removed the Christian churches from their official monopoly, and humanity has breathed more easily from that time onward. Nazism and Communism were thankfully short-lived, and the dogmas in Moslem countries no longer go unquestioned.

The harm done to rulership by the "admixture" religions also harms the love in the world because the need for rulership is like the need for love. If there is order in the world and wisdom in the creation, there is love. When anarchy and chaos prevail, then love hides itself away and waits for its opportunity to come out into the open. All humanity are God's children (the Jews are called "first-born children") because God is like a father to us, loving us when we accept Him and trust His laws.

The prohibition of blasphemy forbids "cursing" God with the use of His name, an act that proclaims rebellious dissatisfaction with His goodness and refuses to return the patience with which He regards us, as His children, when we do wrong. Since God cannot be touched or harmed, the only way that a person feels able to strike back at Him, heaven forbid, is through cursing Him with words. The world was created with divine speech, and it is the human faculty of speech that distinguishes humanity from all other living things, showing that the human being is closest to God and made in His image.

Therefore, the misuse of this faculty, intended as it were to spite the One who granted it, is among the seven main prohibitions to the non-Jewish world. In the Torah, the prohibition is phrased to apply to the Jew and the

non-Jew alike (Lev 24:16). This simultaneous commandment, the only one among the Seven Laws, also indicates
a reference to the concept of Chanukah, in which
non-Jews have a share because Chanukah is an expression of the Sefirah of "Glory" (*Hod*). The completeness
of spiritual victory in this festival comes when both Jews
and non-Jews praise the Creator with their words.

The full court judgment is given only when the
individual uses the divine Name itself or, in non-Jewish
cases, when equivalents such as "Almighty" are used to
formulate a curse against God. However, the law generally forbids using words to denigrate Him in lesser ways,
to compare Him with created entities to His disfavor, and
to speak slightingly of the Torah or its scholars.

All these offenses run counter to faith in God's love
and to the concept of thanking Him and praising Him
even in adverse circumstances. Such offenses deny a faith
in the ultimate good result of all the untoward happenings in our lives. The English word "God" is related to
the word "good," and both of them derive from the
Hebrew name of Gad, the son of Jacob and founder of
one of the twelve Jewish tribes, whose essential concept
was expression and understanding of the divine kindness. In other languages as well, non-Jewish peoples call
God by names that indicate His kindness and love,
showing how necessary it is for all human beings to know
these attributes and to hold fast to them.

The greatest non-Jew who ever lived after the giving
of the Torah was Job, the only non-Jew with a book
named after him in the Torah. He maintained this faith
through adversity, as the foundation of all his righteous
deeds. He was stricken with boils from his head to his
feet as a test of his integrity, and as he sat in pain his

wife scolded him, "Are you still holding to your principles? Curse God and die!"

This was an "invitation" to make himself liable to the full legal penalty for blasphemy. Despite his suffering, Job refused the suggestion to "jump in the lake." His answer was, "'You speak as one who is despicable. Should we accept only the good from Him, and not also accept the evil?' With all this Job did not sin with his lips." (Job 2:9-10).

Beyond the literal meaning of this commandment comes the general concept of "sinning with the lips," meaning all misuse of speech and communication. A person who tells lies, who spreads gossip even if it is true, who uses obscenities (described as the "nakedness of speech"), or who chatters away for nothing is crossing the boundaries that relate the speaking faculty to God and to the divine love in its wider sense.

Included in this definition is deceptive talk that gives rise to false impressions, whether in commercial advertising or political campaigns or in personal relationships. Such deceit causes the loving trust that comes from true words to be diverted and led astray.

It is also inadvisable to "swear" or "vow" to reach goals or make achievements at some moment of crisis, let alone in anger, because these objectives may not be really worthwhile on second thought.

Persons who wish to safeguard themselves from all the traps and dangers into which speech can lead them will realize that none of these false conversations are necessary. It can be fun to talk about other people in an unflattering way or to hear the details of all the things they have been doing lately, but like other fun things it is habit-forming. People want to be aware of what is going on around them and to be considered "in the know," and so they swap items of news that may or may not be relevant to their own lives. A recommendation to watch one's words sounds like an invitation to a monastery, but this is not so. The person who says little will always be considered wise, and others will trust such a person and tell him all that he needs to know.

The prime religious need of any individual is to relate to God through prayer. We are given speech primarily because of God's desire for us to relate to Him in this way. Just as a father loves to hear the words of his child, no matter how garbled or mispronounced the words may be, God is gratified to hear us speak to Him. In fact, because of the heavenly peace that prayer brings, it is possible to say that the only reason He sends us difficulties is to encourage us to pray.

It is also good to say words of Torah in conversation, to enjoy and develop the insights that they contain. As King David wrote (Ps 119:99), "From all who have taught me I have gained wisdom, for Your testimonies are my conversation." One should speak of the Torah's topics with other people on appropriate occasions, in a regular pleasant way, and discuss them in the same way as one discusses one's own affairs, without feeling any hesitation over doing so. It is a great merit to tell other non-Jews about the Seven Laws, and Jews themselves have on many occasions been brought back to the Torah because non-Jews have commented on it to them.

Jews are required to pray communally three times a day, in the morning and afternoon and after nightfall. For this they must gather at least ten adult Jewish men, who stand together facing toward the Temple Mount in Jerusalem and pray the words chosen by the early sages known as the "Men of the Great Assembly," with one of them acting as a leader. Even though they may offer other prayers in any language all day long if they want, they must fulfill this minimum obligation unless it is impossible.

Different prayers are used for the Sabbath and festivals, with the same arrangement. Non-Jews are not obligated to make a quorum or to appoint times, but if they prefer the atmosphere of communal prayer then they may make an assembly at any convenient time or place, as groups who uphold the Seven Laws customarily do. Special prayers have been composed according to the Noachide concepts to help them in this, but they are under no obligation to use them. They must only be prepared to pray, without an intermediary, to God Himself alone, as the Creator of all and the only Being who hears prayer and supplies the wants of humanity.

The prayer of all human beings is an expression of faith. When the lips are used to talk to God in a personal way, addressing Him as the caring and providing source of everything in the world, then faith is upheld. If, however, they are turned to cursing Him, in denial of His true guidance, then faith is damaged and overturned not only for the individual who voices his or her loss of faith but for the world in general.

There is no way to survive the troubles of life without faith because life itself is not destined to be "survived" but to end in death, which is the gateway to heaven. Thus it is only faith in the goodness of life, leading to its reward in the world to come, which makes the troubles bearable and meaningful.

This does not mean that a religiously aware person should surrender to insult and degradation without a word in his or her own cause. There is no need to offer oneself for sacrifice in a quietist or pacifist way, certainly not in the fashion in which Christianity describes the death of its founder and holds it up as an example. No one is obligated to "turn the other cheek" to a mocker or a thief, and one may use such a tactic voluntarily only in the case of insult, not in the case of injury. The Jews killed during the Holocaust in World War II did not offer themselves for murder out of guilt or self-hatred or because they denied the validity of life. Their love of life was great and wholehearted, and their passivity came only from a recognition of God's unfathomable decree at that time. The actions of the Israel Defense Forces in maintaining Jewish security have no spiritual deficiency at all, being the correct expression of the law once the physical means become available.

A person has rights in the law, and so also does the nation, without which the individual would be brought into contempt and suffer loss in his or her life capacity.

American colonists were under no religious obligation to endure the taxation of King George the Third; their protest against his rule was in every way justifiable. Nevertheless, there is a point where one must acknowledge that both the resistible and the impossible situations originate from God's providence itself. Even the Jewish Holocaust, which of all events in history has been the hardest blow to religious security for Jews and non-Jews alike, can only be understood as being above our understanding. "There are more things in heaven and earth than are dreamed of in philosophy," as William Shakespeare wrote, and we must all come to the moment of truth when our ideas resolve themselves into faith for its own sake.

Torah study has the ability to help people develop the capacity for faith that passes these tests much more easily. Those wise in Torah know how to find their way through the many forms of trial that the world offers, recognizing each trial for what it is and treating it accordingly. These are the survivors, the men and women who reach the span of their lives having made the true gains for which they were intended. When people are deprived of Torah education, their innate goodness often enables them to live in this way on a subconscious level and to formulate correct philosophy as well as they can. However, the knowledge of the actual texts can raise this ability to a conscious form where it can take its rightful place at the forefront of attitudes and decisions.

The law against idolatry, because of its relationship to divine rulership, is linked with the purple color in the rainbow. Purple is the royal color, used to show honor and distinction. It is a color of power in its aspect of love, not in its fiery aspect like red. Similarly, the law against blasphemy corresponds to the orange color, warmer than the yellow of the sun but cooler than the red. Orange is the color of warm love, caring and sustaining, innocent and thankful as it reflects different aspects of the colors which are similar to it but do not have its all-embracing nature.

XIV

At first sight, the sixth of the Noachide Laws, the prohibition against eating meat taken from a living animal, seems very different from all of the others. The warnings against theft or murder are linked to issues that touch every one of us at some time, but hardly anyone would consider violating an animal's body to the extent of eating its meat while it was still alive, at least not while normal food is available.

However, the importance of the principle behind this law is not dependent on how frequently its violation occurs in practice. Jewish law requires the eating of "kosher" food, namely substances prepared in such a way that the person does not take into himself or herself anything that comes from a source opposed to truth and kindness. There is a saying that "What you eat, you are," and the Torah therefore tells the non-Jew also that as long as his food has nothing in it which could go against this one condition, then his eating will enhance and sustain his true personal standing. These requirements for Jews and non-Jews have to do with the spiritual constitution and not with physical health or hygiene or any other scientific fact.

This commandment comes sixth in the order of the Sefirot, but it was the last one to be given to humanity. Before the flood, meat of any kind was forbidden as food. After the flood, Noah emerged safely from the ark, and God told him that meat would henceforth be permitted as long as this one condition was maintained in preparing it. The men and women who came out of the ark were clean of the sins of violent robbery and sexual misconduct that had caused the deaths of the rest of humanity, and so this early prohibition was removed from them as long as they kept their eating to meat which carried no trace of those cruel sins. God told Noah, "Only meat with the soul within it, and its blood, shall you not eat" (Gen 9:4), and this completed the Seven Laws that were to be known by Noah's name.

The eating of live meat is at the root source of cruelty and selfishness. People have a rapacious tendency, a desire to take life and to devour it in order to bring their own life to a level of complete reckless indulgence and domination. The connection between eating and sexual intercourse is well-known, and the eating of live meat is connected to the rapacious level of sex, to the kind of intercourse that has no personal contact nor love but merely involves an "eating" of the other person.

This is equally true of the man and of the woman, and sex on this level will give rise to children who are lacking in kindness and consideration from their very origin.

There are few instances of deliberate abuse of this prohibition, but some have been recorded in historic times, and they show very clearly what mentality was at work in those circumstances. In 1770, James Bruce of Kinnaird, Scotland, arrived in Ethiopia. He was one of the first Europeans to visit that remote mountain land,

and he gave a full description of the bizarre doings that he witnessed there. The country was deep in an almost meaningless civil war, with atrocious torture and massacres happening all the time. During the winter season, when fighting was impossible and "lightning ran on the ground like water" from tremendous thunderstorms out of black skies, there would be drunken feasts where live meat was consumed. In *Travels to Discover the Source of the Nile in the Years 1768, 1769, 1770, 1771, 1772, and 1773* (London: Longman and Rees, 1804), Bruce wrote:

> A cow or bull is led into the large hut where the guests are assembled, and when it is tightly secured steaks are hacked from its living flesh. The terrible noise the animal makes is the sign for the company to sit down to table, and before long all are very much elevated. Love lights its fires, and everything is permitted with absolute freedom. There is no coyness, no delays, no need of appointments or retirement to gratify their wishes. There is but one room in which they sacrifice both to Bacchus and to Venus, and if we may judge by sound, they think it as great a shame to make love in silence as to eat. Replaced in their seats again, the company drink the couple's health, and their example is followed at distant ends of the table as each couple fancy. All this passes without remark or scandal, and not even the most distant joke is made upon the transaction.

A few similar practices have been noted elsewhere. The Mongol nomads of Central Asia originally prepared the raw-meat dish known today as steak tartare from living meat and consumed it in much the same circumstances as the Ethiopians above. The United States is not immune from such barbarism. In agricultural areas, after farm animals are castrated, the testicles are sometimes cooked and served as a delicacy called "Rocky Mountain Oysters." These practices might be termed "serious" wrongdoing, without even pretending that the proceedings are going to make anyone happy, and it is easy to see how far normal happiness is from any such pastimes. The Mongol nomads and Ethiopians ate the living meat raw, showing that they were not looking for food gratification, and they did so because it contained the "heat of life," the element that inflames selfish passions and degrades the personal level of relationships. This kind of eating is prohibited in the main Seven Laws, showing that it is a major offense on a level with theft and bloodshed and that it closely resembles both of these.

The Sefirah of Kindness, the first in the order of Sefirot, is concerned with forbidden partnerships, but this law relates to the quality of the intercourse itself, the way in which the couple relate to each other while they are together. The sixth Sefirah is known as *Yesod* or "Foundation." In the scheme of the human body, it parallels the male reproductive organ, which renews the generations and provides the "foundation" for their makeup and attitudes as they are born. The non-Jew rectifies his sexual drive and brings it to the level required of it by avoiding any meat that transgresses the prohibition against eating living meat even accidentally, according to the details specified by the Torah.

The eating of living meat is forbidden to Jews also, but their law only forbids them from eating the living meat of kosher animals, while the non-Jews are forbidden the meat of all land creatures not fully dead. The non-Jewish law considers an animal as dead only when all its limbs have stopped moving, whereas in Jewish law the stroke of the knife across the throat in the ritual method of slaughter renders the animal legally dead from that moment. The majority opinion is that an animal slaughtered for Jews is permitted to the non-Jew even though its limbs have not stopped moving because the law of Jewish slaughter excludes the non-Jewish prohibition entirely.

Therefore, a non-Jew who eats meat slaughtered by another non-Jew has to be sure that the animal was not cut up for meat before its limbs stopped moving. In the busy world of today's mechanized slaughterhouses, this is by no means always so. Much of the meat sold in non-Jewish stores is at risk from this point of view, and therefore many observers of the Seven Laws avoid meat entirely and live as vegetarians, even though they are not required to do this. If they live in areas where Jewish meat is available, then they eat only that, both at home and in restaurants.

In this way they maintain themselves and their children spiritually as the law enjoins them to do. Our society has formed the habit of handling its meat animals quickly and carelessly, without knowledge of the effects that this can cause, and the rise in its level of sexual selfishness can likewise be seen. If this troublesome aspect of modern life was linked to its main cause, then people would be liberated from its effects, free to rise to a much more confident level in their personal relations. This is the only food prohibition for non-Jews, but it still needs care and attention in order to safeguard the new generations of children as they are brought into the world.

This law was one of the topics in the dispute recorded in the Book of Genesis (37:2) between Joseph and his brothers, which caused them to sell him into slavery in Egypt. He maintained that they were forbidden to eat the meat of an animal whose limbs were still moving because they were at this time bound by the Seven Laws. His brothers took the view that they were allowed to observe the Jewish law, which permitted such an animal immediately after the ritual slaughter, because they were engaged in producing the children who would become the Jewish people and be given the whole Torah.

Joseph had had a dream with prophetic content, and his position on the legal ruling was based upon it. His brothers considered him too young to reach the prophetic level. Thus they judged him to be disputing the rabbinic authority that they represented, and they discussed among themselves whether this made him liable to the death penalty or only to be sold as a slave. In the end, they adopted the more lenient view, and Joseph was sold into Egypt, where God raised him to be ruler of the land after he resisted his master's wife in her attempt to induce him to break the Seven Laws by having relations with her. His brothers then came to bow before him as the dream had predicted, thus confirming that he had been correct in the position he had originally taken.

There is an opinion that the food animals of non-Jews must be slaughtered, but the ruling decision is that they may eat the meat of an animal that has died by itself. However, this is better avoided. Fish are permitted as food to both Jews and non-Jews from the moment the fish leave the water, and the non-Jew is not penalized for eating meat from a living bird even though this is forbidden. Eating meat from a slaughtered animal whose limbs are still moving also does not incur the penalty, though this practice is forbidden.

Eating even a tiny amount of living flesh, whether cooked or raw, violates the prohibition. It is forbidden to cause any damage to a living animal that leaves a portion of flesh hanging down from an attachment; even when this is caused by an accident the flesh may not simply be cut away and eaten. If the wound is so serious that it would not be possible to restore the flesh to position and allow the animal to live for a year, then the hanging portion is considered as "living meat" and remains forbidden even after immediate slaughter. A broken tip does not invalidate the whole of the rest of the limb, but if most of the flesh of any limb is missing, then the whole limb must be removed after slaughter before any of the animal's meat can be eaten.

The Talmud records a dispute among the rabbis as to whether non-Jews are permitted to eat or drink blood that has been drawn from a living animal, something that is forbidden to Jews. This is the regular practice among nomadic tribes in East Africa, such as the Masai, because their pasturage is scarce and they find it too expensive to kill their cattle for food. Therefore, they draw blood from a neck vein without causing distress to the animal, just as veterinarians do, and they mix it with the milk to make a rich broth which can be drunk raw or cooked until it congeals for eating.

The question behind the dispute is whether the blood of the animal contains the "heat of life" while it is circulating in the vein or while present in the flesh itself. Most of the early authorities agree that blood present in meat is spiritually harmful to the non-Jew, even if the meat was not taken from the living animal, but that blood has only a limited life-character during its time of transfer to and from the heart. Therefore, the Masai practice would be seen as not harmful.

All the food prohibitions in the Torah, whether for Jews or non-Jews, have deep mystical significance concerning the transmigration of souls and the ultimate destiny of every living creature until the redemption.

Since all of the animal world was given over to humanity, it follows that the meaning of animals' lives has to do with their relationship to human beings. Nowhere is this clearer than with food animals whose flesh we absorb into our own being. Animals do not possess the true intellectual soul given to the human being, shown by the human face and upright posture and the faculty of rational understanding. Animal intelligence exists on an emotional level only, and they see people as being above themselves in closeness to God for this reason.

Therefore animals feel a need to reach their true destiny through the help of people, and for food animals this means being eaten according to the laws of the Torah. All living things must die, and just as a person desires integrity in death through proper burial of the body that once housed his or her soul, so an animal seeks consummation through being absorbed into the higher human order as food, without any reluctance or misunderstanding. However, human disregard of the Torah impedes this process, whether it is a Jew eating a forbidden animal or a non-Jew eating the meat in its state of "blood" as the Torah proscribes.

Jewish ritual slaughter of a permitted animal removes the soul in the correct spiritual manner for Jews, and slaughter by any humane means readies the meat for consumption by non-Jews as soon as all signs of life have passed away. These laws show us that our eating of animal food is not intended solely for our own gratification but as a service to the whole created world, even to the foods that the animals themselves have eaten, rectifying it and bringing its spirituality to completion in ourselves.

In these ways we adjust our eating to the needs of the whole mysterious universes of plant and animal life, which are otherwise far beyond our understanding because the mercy and goodness of the Torah reach above the highest worlds. These also are aspects of the Sefirah of Foundation.

This law corresponds to the green color in the rainbow, the color of plants and leaves, as befitting its relevance to human seed and to the foundation of the food chain that sustains all life for the present and the future. When our cruelty is rectified, its power becomes healthy and good like the green leaves, and as the leaves have become a symbol for environmental concern so they show the way to moderating the passions that lead to waste and destruction.

XV

Though the Seven Laws do not exist in order to punish people, there would be no point in calling them "laws" at all if there were no courts to enforce them when necessary. Every society since the dawn of time has recognized that there are people who yield to the impulse to break the law and that law has no value, in anyone's eyes, if it is not enforced.

The idea that laws are repressive and harmful—and that people will find their way if left to themselves—is deeply mistaken and leads to every possible abuse and degradation. The world itself is harmed in its essence when such an idea, even when based on good and unselfish motives, is put into practice. The Seven Laws bear witness to this in the final commandment, which is derived from the same source that affirms divine rulership by prohibiting idolatry. The sages interpret the word "commanded" in Genesis 2:16 ("And the Lord God commanded it upon the man") to mean that human beings are to maintain these commandments through appropriate means, namely through the establishment of courts of justice.

This law is represented also by the last of the Sefirot, which corresponds to the feet. The feet have the most lowly function of all but give their support to the other parts of the body, including the head itself, maintaining them in their high positions. This Sefirah has the name of *Malchut* or "Sovereignty." Even though a king is greatly honored and respected, his inner nature is to do the lowest and most humble of all work, serving the public good with total lack of regard for his own well being.

This is the way that the law should be run, in truth and sincerity, without any thought other than the good of humanity according to the wishes of the Creator. When the law and its upholders have the attitudes they need for this, then the whole structure of social relations leaves error and wrongdoing far behind. Most of today's governments are considered to be upholding this commandment on a basic level, even though they hardly know of the Seven Laws, because their inner motivation is to do what God wants in this way.

However, when justice becomes so corrupt that this commandment no longer has any standing in society, or when the legal system gives punishments for actions that are legal under the Seven Laws, then the situation enters into constitutional illegality.

Societies like these are legitimate targets for thorough change, and those who rule them may be defeated and put on trial. Such governments abuse the trust placed in them as emissaries of the Almighty, and they make themselves liable to be judged in their turn. When courts are of so little account that private scores can only be settled through vendettas, then the locality is in breach of the requirement. There is likewise no validity to any tradition that permits vendettas in place of a regular system of law.

In criminal cases the basic code of law for non-Jewish states consists of the Seven Laws themselves, but in civil matters non-Jews are not required to follow the law of the Torah as laid down in the Book of Exodus, chapters 21-23. They make their own laws as they see fit, in accordance with equitable principles, and appoint their own judges to settle cases according to the particular need of each nation. The only requirement in civil matters is that they allow Jews to live according to the full extent of Torah law without being judged in any other way.

The nations are not commanded to enthrone kings as the Jews are, and so they may have any form of government they wish. They can form a republic or a monarchy, a unitary state or a federal system, as long as the government rules over the whole territory without breaking the Seven Laws and as long as it appoints judges to hear both civil and criminal proceedings in every locality. For example, the national government makes laws setting out the terms on which people may establish corporations. When those terms are fulfilled, the corporation exists only through the government's power of laws which gave the means of creating it. Therefore, anyone who steals the property of a corporation is not breaking the prohibition of theft but only the commandment to uphold the power of laws vested in the government. Police arrangements that prevent crime instead of investigating and making arrests after the fact are not a legal necessity in themselves, but they become an obligation if this is the only the way the judiciary can be maintained. There must also be a corps of bailiffs and other officers who carry out the verdicts of the court once they are delivered.

These provisions do not apply to any part of the land of Israel; its purpose is to serve as the source of constitutional morality and the jurisdictional center for the Jewish people and the Torah applicable to them. When this principle is established, then the land of Israel is seen in its true relationship to other lands, which benefit their non-Jewish inhabitants through the Seven Laws that are taught and strengthened from there. When non-Jews reside in the Holy Land, under any circumstances, the Seven Laws provide the basis on which the Jews will relate to them and judge them.

This commandment at first seems to be an affirmative commandment, an instruction to do something, rather than a prohibition like the other six commandments. However, its real intent is to forbid the offense of failing to set up courts, of breaking the laws duly made for the purposes of social order, of leaving offenders unpunished and litigants without recourse to justice.

This failure is the factor that damages the world and harms its relationship with God, and so the Torah penalizes it in order to uphold the principle of justice, which states that anyone who judges a case according to its truth becomes a partner with God Himself in making the world.

When this is done, the merit is shared by every individual in the locality, not only by the judge himself; when it is not done, every private individual shares in the penalty.

Until recently, most governments in the world were monarchies, and so the word "court," which denoted the personal surroundings of the king, came to mean a place where justice is made available. This is because the function of judges was to act as expert deputies for the king by carrying out his personal function of hearing pleas and giving out legal decisions. Even in republican states, the judges sit only in the name of the true sovereign power, however it is defined, exercising its sole legitimate right of adjudication. The judge who hears a case fully and decides it impartially, according to the law, is considered a partner with God Himself in the entire creation because he is using the sovereign authority with which the creation was made.

Non-Jewish courts may convict on the testimony of one witness, even a relative of the defendant if he or she has no bias, and before a single judge. Neither of these conditions is true for Jews. Justice must be rendered in the duly authorized court, not by private committees or vigilante tribunals. If a court case can be avoided by seeking arbitration or compromise, it is meritorious to do so, but once the courts have heard the pleas, their decision is final and must be accepted.

It is obligatory to give whatever testimony one knows, even if it will convict a friend or acquit an enemy. In criminal cases, one must come forward to testify even if the court does not issue a request to do so because of the divine relevance and standing of the Seven Laws, which incorporate God's own knowledge of all circumstances.

Neither wicked people nor anyone who would benefit from the decision nor the husband of any woman involved in the proceedings may give evidence or sit as judges. The only evidence admitted is direct personal witness to events, including circumstantial happenings, not hearsay evidence of any kind. A false witness who brings about another's execution is himself liable to the death penalty.

A non-Jew who breaks one of the Seven Laws unintentionally is not penalized at all, in contrast to a Jew who in many cases must bring a sacrifice to atone for inadvertent sins. However, this applies only when, for instance, a non-Jewish man has intercourse with a woman believing that she is permitted to him when in fact she is in a forbidden category. If he knows her category but does not know that such a woman is forbidden, or if he is under the impression that the prohibition does not apply to him, then he is not called an unintentional transgressor. In these circumstances, he has the responsibility of finding out for himself what the law says. For the same reason, there is no need for non-Jews to be warned before an offense because the Seven Laws are close enough to common sense and human decency to make non-Jewish individuals liable even if they are not taught them.

When non-Jews are forced by others under pain of death to transgress the Seven Laws, they are permitted to commit the offense and save themselves. They may even worship idols in these circumstances. Only the Jews are commanded to "sanctify the Name" by undergoing martyrdom for its commandments. Neither children, the mentally challenged, nor the deaf and dumb can be punished legally under any circumstances.

The authorities differ over when non-Jews reach the age of legal majority; some say that their ages are the same as those for the Jews, namely twelve years for girls and thirteen for boys. Others maintain that the age when they achieve full understanding, whether younger or older than the standard definitions, serves as the legal minimum.

The judge's responsibility is great, and a person needs high qualifications to undertake the task. Judges must be brave and independent-minded so as to be without fear of the consequences of what they decide, especially if they are likely to be threatened. They must be wise and humble, fearing God as the One who judges them in their turn, and they must actively turn from financial gain in their personal lives. They must love truth, fear to do wrong, and have good reputations that make them beloved by their fellows.

People may not judge either their friends or their enemies, even if they are not close as friends or bitter as enemies. They should not help either of the litigants with their cases or speak in a different way to one of them. Rather, they should remain silent and hear out all that each litigant has to say. If a litigant or a witness becomes upset or flustered, the judge may help the person out and put him or her on the right track again, but this must be done carefully so as not to pervert the course of the trial. Judges must never be haughty or give their decisions without duly considering all the aspects of the case.

When more than one judge is sitting, it is forbidden for any one of them to reveal how he or the others had assessed or voted in the verdict.

Judges may not accept bribes, even to convict the guilty or acquit the innocent. This is true no matter how small the bribe or how indirect. For example, a judge who receives rent due from a tenant before the regular date is disqualified because this can be understood as a bribe. Judges who make mistaken judgments in financial cases are not obligated to return the damages because their character qualifications make it clear that they have no intention to cause harm.

Because the divine commandment to the nations of the world is specifically to attend to the functioning of justice, we see that all of world government with its social mechanisms exists primarily to carry out this single function. There is no direct commandment to raise taxes, to pay out Social Security, to maintain military forces, or to send ambassadors abroad for the purpose of conducting diplomacy. These aspects of government are intended to keep the judicial system working and to protect it from all dangers. The judicial system is the only basis for the proper adjustment of social relations.

When rulers do not attend to a proper judicial system—for instance, when they try to make themselves the sole authority in order to make profit from the people—then they are offenders against the law and must be removed. The English Civil War in the seventeenth century was fought over the question of whether the king, Charles the First, was in violation of the fundamental principles of this law. He tried to place himself above it by invoking a higher right belonging only to him as a king. He raised taxes unconstitutionally, and citizens could not be sure what the law was from one occasion to the next or how they would be judged in court. Charles claimed that his position as a king gave him an absolutist right to rule on the basis of principles existing in his mind alone.

The English Parliament defeated his forces in battle, put him on trial, and executed him for this offense. The parliamentary leaders then began negotiations with Jewish rabbinic leaders in Holland to allow the Jews to settle in England. This was intended, among other things, to show to the world that the king's execution had not been an act of rebellion but was in accordance with the law of the Torah. The Seven Laws, which the Dutch in particular had promoted, had become an important means of state advancement. The abolition of the medieval prohibition on interest-bearing loans, according to the Seven Laws, was the key change which enabled the Dutch to finance their technical advancement and the extension of their sea-trading empire. The English were eager to take the process even further.

At that time kings were very much respected and feared, and one had to be on solid ground before executing one of them. Their absolute rulership was held by many to be the visible presence of God on earth, and their persons were considered sacred, far above their subjects' ideas of propriety. The Tsar of Russia broke off diplomatic relations with England because of the execution, and the King of France threatened war against them. Later he launched a full-scale land attack on the Dutch because of their freedoms and was beaten back in a desperate struggle.

If the Jews had placed their decision behind the absolutist view, it would have spelled disaster for the English in the face of such powerful forces. Jewish support would never have been given to Parliament if King Charles had been innocent according to the Seven Laws.

The English also offered the Jews a share in their growing overseas empire, especially in the new land of America, assuring them that Torah law would be present as a founding principle there. The readmission of the Jews to England was intended to precede their admission to America in due time, which was being established in a manner acceptable to Jews, closer to Torah and the Seven Laws than the monarchies of Europe and Russia had been.

As a new land, America needed a new set of practical concepts to make it accessible. An abstract legal entity unknown in the Middle Ages, the joint-stock company, proved the only means of establishing colonies so far across the ocean. The new acceptability of Torah learning among non-Jews led to the devising of this specific arrangement for shared long-distance enterprise. The Dutch West India Company founded the city of New Amsterdam on this basis, and Jews were among the stockholders and directors of the company for the first time in any European enterprise. When the English captured the city and renamed it New York, the Jews who had settled there brought this Dutch arrangement into the British system on a permanent basis.

These changes in favor of the rule of law later led the American founders to adopt the principle of "judicial review," which gave the Supreme Court the power to uphold or overturn legislation. This power gives the ultimate guarantee to the American Constitution and shows how the supremacy of law lies at the heart of all properly constituted government in the non-Jewish world, according to the divine intention.

It was men like Grotius and Selden who pioneered these arrangements in their writings, who knew how to read and understand the Jewish sources, and who were at home with learned Jews as colleagues and friends.

Though we are required to make an effort to see that justice is done, there will always be cases where it is impossible to bring a matter to trial. Evidence from valid witnesses may be lacking or the claimant may not wish to testify to everything he or she knows. Many kinds of doubt can arise that render human judgment unreliable. Countries that have abolished the death penalty for murder are following this evidential rule; modern society is so complex and confused that firm evidence is hard to come by, and no court can take a human life in circumstances that are doubtful in any way.

Therefore, we must realize that the Almighty never gives up on His own justice for the world. He arranges events in His wisdom so that an unpunished murderer happens to stay in a hotel that catches fire or so that a thief loses everything on the stock market during a crash. If punishments are needed, He exacts them Himself, with no escape from His territory. In all the terrible events that can happen in the world, we can be sure that God weighs the case of every person involved, showing mercy to those whom He chooses and showing judgment to those who deserve it. Since our human faculties often are unable to try these cases in the courts we have, it is obvious that the criteria being used in His judgment are far above and beyond our understanding.

This is the concept of the Jewish New Year, Rosh Hashanah, the anniversary of the creation of the first man and woman. On Rosh Hashanah, God sits as King in His court and judges each and every one of us, Jew and non-Jew, with His complete knowledge and understanding. The prayer composed for the day expresses the idea with great beauty:

> Let us tell of the holiness of this day, and of its awesome power.
>
> On this day Your rule shall be exalted, Your throne established in mercy, and You shall occupy it in truth.
>
> You open the book of all records, and it reads itself; every man's signature is within it.
>
> As a shepherd seeks out his flock, making the sheep pass under his rod, so do You count and number Your creatures, fixing their lifetime, establishing their destiny.
>
> On the New Year their destiny is inscribed...how many shall pass away, and how many be brought into existence;
>
> who shall live and who shall die; who in good time and who untimely...
>
> who shall have comfort and who shall be tormented; who shall become poor and who shall become wealthy;
>
> who shall be lowered, and who shall be raised.

The prayer is directed toward arousing the heart to repentance and prayer because only by this means can we influence the decree of the day in our favor. Even so, this is not a day of tears or despair. We know that the Almighty loves all His creatures and desires only to do good for them, and so this day is a festival despite its awesome character. Non-Jews do not observe the ritual rest of the day or eat the obligatory meals, but they join in the realization of what is happening, and they make their personal accounting with its concepts in whatever way they choose.

This last commandment corresponds to the "dark" color of the rainbow, often called brown because it is the color of the earth from which all life emerges and to which it returns. This is the humble color, chosen by those who wish to be inconspicuous, the color that emerges from the blending of all the different elements that make up fertile soil. Though brown has no emotional value of its own, it serves as the point of departure for all the others, the standard by which they are measured and the reality underlying them all.

XVI

I n addition to the seven basic laws, the non-Jewish nations are given a number of overall principles and supplementary commandments that do not fall under court jurisdiction.

The non-Jew must acknowledge the unity of the Creator. He is realized to be Creator in the sense that nothing created Him and that He has no element of multiplicity that would give Him separateness or distinction like the created beings. There is no distinction between Him and His knowledge as there is in the human being and no change in Him from before He made the creation.

This last fact is responsible for one of the greatest paradoxes of all existence: if there is no change in Him now that He has created the world, then how indeed has He created it if only He has true existence? The true answer is that, relative to Him, the world has not been created at all and that everything is still as it was before the creation. He has only given it the appearance of existence in order to provide human beings with the environment that He desires for them.

Thus we see the realization that appears in many eastern religions and that has gained influence in the west as a counterweight to the scientific view that takes existence as an absolute fact. Our perceptions tell us, when we analyze them clearly, that the world is made up of both being and nothingness, existence and dissolution. The Seven Laws require the non-Jew to acknowledge this as originating from the Creator's own unity itself.

There is also an obligation to see truth as the only key to the revelation of the human soul and to understanding the purpose of created life in this world. Many people claim that truth does not matter so much or that it is all right for those who care to find out about it. To this, we would have to respond that living on such a level misses the vital element for which life was intended and that, however much people have become accustomed to living without truth, it can never be dispensed with altogether.

The Seven Laws have to be accepted and obeyed because they are divine commandments given to human beings through prophecy and not because they appear logical or necessary to us on their own. They can certainly be understood as beautiful and intelligent because their purpose is not to lead us out of our senses into unworldly surroundings where the normal perceptions fail us, but this understanding only follows from accepting the divine origin of the commandments and keeping them accordingly.

This acceptance restrains the non-Jew from creating a new religion, even one based on the Seven Laws, because one then understands that the human sense of morality can never improve upon the laws given to Moses from on high.

Human rulership over animal life is likewise an obligatory realization. Some say that animals have greater purity and integrity than humans and that we should try to live as they do. However, human deficiency exists only because of free will, and the animals appear superior to us only when we make bad moral choices. A person who keeps God's laws will never feel inferior to an animal. Moreover, that person will be ready and capable of ruling over the animal world in its own best interests. From this we understand how the Seven Laws can provide solutions to such problems as endangered species and to environmental problems in general.

Other supplementary commandments concerning animals forbid the castration of males and the deliberate cross-breeding of different species. These have long been standard practices in agriculture, and most farmers would find it inconvenient to abandon them. Nevertheless, the Seven Laws exclude them specifically, not because they are more cruel than other permitted practices but because they confuse and obstruct the divine order in nature in a significant way, harming the animal order along with our own. They are not punishable by the courts, but the hand of heaven exacts retribution according to the exact weighing of each circumstance, as is always the case where the offense cannot be tried before earthly judges for any reason.

Non-Jews are not commanded to honor their parents, but from the earliest times they have taken it upon themselves to do so as an obligation. In this area they are said to excel the Jews, who are commanded to do so, and this is an example of what the non-Jewish nature can accomplish. Because a parent is a partner with God in the creating of a person, one should honor and respect one's parents much as one honors and respects God, out of gratitude for having been created and born.

Parents should not be ousted from their place or contradicted. When they grow old, they must be fed and clothed and accommodated—from the child's own funds if the parents have no money of their own. This is true even if the parent is a wicked person or has not fulfilled parental obligations. However, a parent who causes harm may be resisted like any other individual, though with somewhat more caution because they are presumed to have good intentions.

Parents do not need to insist on their honor, and they are better advised to set it aside wherever possible and live in a friendly and informal manner. Of course, the most honorable thing for parents to do is to raise their children and teach them according to the Seven Laws. Nothing brings more honor on parents than the example of children who live good and upright lives.

The true nature of all humanity is to do good and, in the event of having sinned, to repent and return to God. This urge is so great that those who try to act as if nothing were required of them will feel disquiet and unease within themselves, even though the surrounding world encourages them to deny what they are feeling. Sometimes they will try to compensate half-consciously. There are instances of people returning to undergo punishment for their crimes in order to merit forgiveness. One such person was the Irish playwright Oscar Wilde, a highly-talented man who let his life slide deeply into sexual and financial immorality but who refused a chance to flee the country when charged with his offense. He remained behind to stand trial and face imprisonment after realizing where his vanity had led him.

Every original society on earth has a belief of some kind in a supernatural order. Recently, there has been an increase in the desire to relate to the mystical side of life, as found in the Kabbalah or in other ideas which lead to it, and this testifies to the existence and to the strength of the spiritual element in the human constitution. There are many examples of this yearning for fulfillment, sometimes in the form of organized religion, sometimes in love relationships or in stories about them, sometimes in the desire for true knowledge and for justice. They are all parts of the same effort to reach out beyond oneself and relate to the divine.

These yearnings can only go part of the distance toward fulfillment as long as they are not predicated on the reason why we are given laws and precepts to follow. The Seven Laws are not merely a way to find happiness, even true happiness, and still less just a useful means of keeping people in line. They cannot be understood until we take cognizance of the way in which they relate to ultimate purposes. And this cognizance rests on understanding the workings of the divine providence, the workings of the world toward its destined goal, as manifested in the lives of each and every one of us.

A world abandoned to natural laws would be dull and boring beyond belief. No novel or movie would ever have the power to gain people's attention and reveal to them the mystery of the Hand that guides their lives. The human element in its happenings is the divine element, raising and lowering, impoverishing and enriching, to each individual in so deep and significant a fashion as to be the marrow of life itself. We all know how the world is far from perfect, yet we may remain unaware of how much wisdom lies behind its imperfection. Any fool could run a perfect world; he would just set everything up and keep the wheels pointing in the right direction. Only God Himself can run an imperfect world. Only He can organize the world's events down to the smallest detail so that its workings and values are preserved—and its destiny is accomplished.

With all the immorality in the world, it is a cause for wonder that its foundations do not collapse altogether in short order. The fact that it does not do so points straight to the origin of its moral basis. The merit of Noah in his time secured from God the promise that wrongdoing would never gain the upper hand, and the Seven Laws given to him were the testimony to that promise. Noah was the ancestor of all human beings, with their great range of talents and colors of the skin, and as such he was the originator of all good and noble character in the world of today, wherever it is to be found.

When people see that the world is not made for food and drink, sex, money, or power—and they regret how they once thought it was—they reach the point of contact with this moral order that their ancestor Noah established for them. They actualize their own potential for good, and in that moment they change the divine providence affecting them from one meant for a person on a certain kind of level to one meant for another kind of person. All of creation will then move over by divine command to give them the conditions they need to realize the potential for good within them. Because of them the world itself becomes a different place.

If many people were to do this on the basis of the Seven Laws, these changes would come to the forefront of public attention. There would be a decrease in violence and cruelty of all kinds and a rise in benevolence and kindness, all resulting from the great clarity of knowledge and insight that the Torah provides. The reduction in aimlessness and confusion would affect the lives of everyone.

When law is properly established in non-Jewish states, the world's order is assured. Criminals who attempt to escape or corrupt the law, or rulers who seize power with illegal ideas, produce a state of disorder where individuals are denied all their human rights in other countries besides those directly affected. This is the state of spiritual exile, where truth and love retreat to hiding places, unavailable for the happy and fulfilled life of wisdom and peace.

The rabbis say that war comes to the world through the delaying of justice, through the perversion of justice, and for teaching Torah not in accordance with its legal character. Our generation, which has seen such a great upsurge in the longing for peace, can now understand how peace is really to be achieved. We can reach the goal so long denied to humanity while the Torah's exile had to be endured. We are standing on the brink of the Messianic redemption itself, when true law will once again "go forth from Jerusalem," bringing justice and peace to all the nations of the world and uniting them in God's praise as one.

This eventual redemption is foretold in all the prophetic writings of the Torah, and the Jews have always obeyed the legal ruling to regard it as the keystone of their faith and to await it each and every day. Now the nations of the world also are becoming aware of their role in this. They no longer regard Jewish life as at cross-purposes with their own, but they share in the same hopes and expectations. All of humanity has suffered through the exile, continuing to do so even today, and all will share in the reward.

The Torah was not given so that it would remain forever subject to difficulty and misinterpretation. In the very fact of having been given, with its provision for both Jews and non-Jews, it held the necessity that at some time it would be kept perfectly and honored according to its due.

The work of the exile is now all but completed, and Jews and non-Jews are ready to behold the glory of the Torah and its laws here on earth, without want or difficulty, without injustice, war or crime. In that day, says the prophet Zephaniah, "[God] will turn to the nations in a clear language, that they may all call upon the Name of the Lord, to serve Him with one voice" (Zeph 3:9).

Soon the Seven Laws will no longer be kept by a minority like the Godfearers of Roman times. Soon they will not be known only to a few individuals like Aimé Pallière. The reality of Noah's Ark as a predecessor of the former Temples also places it on the level of the Third Temple, the final redemptive structure that will be the heart of the Messianic age. At that time God will "remember the covenant with Noah" so that the "waters of Noah" should not go forth for destruction in any sense of the term (Is 54:9). Then the ingathering will bring all the nations to know and understand the Seven Laws, as the inheritance destined for them. They will live in harmony as God intended and benefit from His wisdom in all its purity, "for the world will be filled with the knowledge of God as the waters cover the ocean bed" (Is 11:9), and the message of this book only a foretaste of what is to come.

> Praise the Lord, all nations; extol Him, all the peoples (Ps 117:1).

> Blessed is God forever, Amen and Amen.

SOURCES

The "Seven Laws for the descendants of Noah" are based on Biblical passages, as has been explained, and they are expounded in detail by the rabbis in the Jerusalem Talmud, Tractate "Kiddushin," and the Babylonian Talmud, Tractate "Sanhedrin," chapter 7. Other explanations are to be found in:

Tosefta Avodah Zarah 9:4

Genesis Rabbah 16:9

Deuteronomy Rabbah 2:17

Maimonides, Laws of Kings chapters 8-10

Modern sources include:

Benamozeg, Rabbi Elijah. *Israël et Humanité*. Paris: Ernest Levoux, 1914.

Clorfene, Chaim, and Yaakov Rogalsky. *The Path of the Righteous Gentile*. Southfield, Michigan: Targum Press, 1987.

Hirsch, Rabbi Samson Rafael. *Horeb*. New York: Soncino Press, 1994.

———. *Nineteen Letters*. Jerusalem: Feldheim Publishers, Ltd., 1995.

Lichtenstein, Aaron. *The Seven Laws of Noah*. New York: Rabbi Jacob Joseph School Press, 1981.

Mozeson, Isaac E. *The Word: Dictionary of the Hebrew Sources of English.* New York: Shapolsky Publishers, 1989.

Pallière, Aimé. *The Unknown Sanctuary.* Translated by Louise Waterman Wise. New York: Block Publishing Co, 1928.

Schwartz, Rabbi Yoel. *A Light unto the Nations.* Jerusalem: Dvar Yerushalayim Publications, 1988.

Talmudic opinions are given to the effect that the individual precepts included under the seven general headings number either sixty-six or thirty.

INDEX
OF SUBJECTS

INDEX
OF TORAH REFERENCES